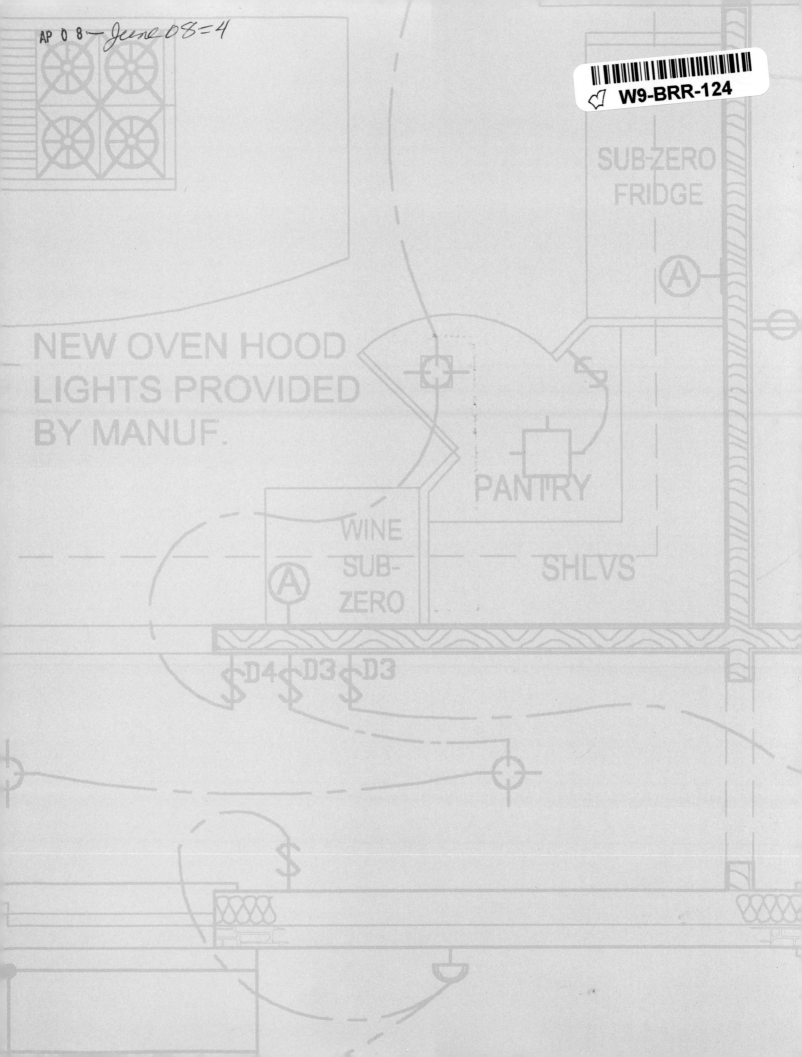

AP 08— June 08=4

NEW OVEN HOOD
LIGHTS PROVIDED
BY MANUF.

SUB-ZERO
FRIDGE

Ⓐ

PANTRY

WINE
SUB-
ZERO

Ⓐ

SHLVS

$D4 $D3 $D3

$

LYN PETERSON'S
Real Life
Kitchens

LYN PETERSON'S
Real Life
Kitchens

Clarkson Potter/Publishers
New York

All rights reserved.
Published in the United States by Clarkson Potter/Publishers, an imprint of the Crown
Publishing Group, a division of Random House, Inc., New York.
www.crownpublishing.com
www.clarksonpotter.com

Clarkson N. Potter is a trademark and Potter and colophon are registered
trademarks of Random House, Inc.

Library of Cataloging-in-Publication Data
Peterson, Lyn.
Lyn Peterson's real life kitchens / Lyn Peterson.
Includes index.
1. Kitchens—Remodeling.   I. Title.   II. Real life kitchens.
TH4816.3.K58.P477   2007
747.7'97—dc22   2007002763

ISBN 978-0-307-35162-3

Printed in China

Design by Jennifer K. Beal

All photographs by Robert Grant except photographs on pages ii, iii,
21, and 214 by Allan Carlisle; pages 6, 8, 20, 104, 120 (top), 217, and 224 by Veronica
Romano-Cagliero; pages 22 (top), 25 (top), 30 (far left), 34, 35, 38, 44, 45, 46, 48, 51, 60
(bottom), 69, 70, 71, 80, 82 (right), 83, 92, 96, 110, 114, 115, 120 (bottom), 128, 129, 145,
146, 156, 157, 159, 161, 162, 163, 165 (bottom), 170, 192, 196 (right), 199, 201, 209, 210,
211, 216, 218, 219, 220, 222, 223, and 235 by Mick Hales; pages 26 (top), 124, and 125
by Walter Elliott; pages 148, 149, and 150 by Diana McMahon.

10 9 8 7 6 5 4 3 2 1

First Edition

To all of my decorating customers for lending me their kitchens and teaching me so much about how our generation wants to cook, live, and spend time at home— thank you.

contents

the surfaces

the lighting

auxiliary spaces

survival guide

Introduction

Kitchens feed us in more ways than one. The best ones tap our creativity, nurture a sense of family, and set the tone for the whole aesthetic of the home. On any given day, we spend more waking time in the kitchen than any other room of the house. Why not bring our own decorative taste into the mix so our kitchen reflects personality as well as function? If my kitchen weren't as pleasing to the eye as it is efficient, I am not sure it would sate my appetite for living.

Real Life Kitchens is a testament to the idea of a room that is both pragmatic and stylish. After all, a kitchen's purpose now extends far beyond cooking and eating to include working, studying, socializing, or simply hanging out and relaxing. To accommodate this broader role, today's kitchens are, on average, 25 percent larger than just a decade ago, and all the "fixings" have grown in size and number, too. Along with the usual ranges and refrigerators, kitchens now accommodate less usual appliances such as steam ovens, wine coolers, and warming drawers as well as formerly living room–style furnishings; my own kitchen has three upholstered chairs, an ottoman, a rug or two, many lamps, a sideboard, and a blanket chest. Add a few nonculinary technological necessities like computers, CD/DVD players, and TVs, and you have established the true core of the house, the center of activity, creativity, and communication. No wonder the kitchen ranks as the most requested of all renovations. As rooms in a house go, the kitchen takes a lot and also gives a lot back.

The kitchen, not coincidentally, is also the most costly space to renovate, when you add up the high prices of construction, cabinetry, stone, and appliances. With big money comes big decisions—and, often, big angst. There's a sense of permanence unique to kitchen renovations that adds fuel to the anxiety. Unlike a living room, in which you might decide to slide the sofa over or shift the piano, a kitchen consists of immovable objects: cabinetry bracketed to the wall, appliances hooked up to gas and water lines, an island anchored to the floor—all the more reason to come up with a carefully conceived plan before installation.

To help you navigate a kitchen project, I've laid out a realistic, doable, and, I hope, inspirational guide. The book starts with the big picture—what you envision your kitchen to be—and segues to the nuts and bolts: drafting the layout; choosing appliances, cabinetry, countertops, flooring, and lighting; and, finally, assembling the team that will make it all happen. (For a detailed timeline, see "The Overall Order," on the following page). To further illuminate the process, I've consulted

THE OVERALL ORDER

- Define your needs/goals.
- Set a budget.
- Draw up plans with the help of architects and/or kitchen designers (the drafting process can take three weeks or more, depending on the complexity of the job).
- File for building permits (this can take up to a month).
- While the permits are being reviewed, solicit bids from three or more contractors (it typically takes three weeks for bids to be returned).
- Check references and select a contractor.
- Order materials: The lead time for cabinets is 12 to 16 weeks; for appliances, 2 to 8 weeks; for stone for counters, 2 to 6 weeks; for tile, 2 to 8 weeks.
- Once the foundation and framing go up first, install windows, plumbing, electrical wiring, heating, venting, and air-conditioning ductwork, followed by insulation, Sheetrock, and exterior siding.

For more information on putting your team together, see "Survival Guide," page 215.

- Prepare floors; add a plywood underlayment, if needed.
- Prepare walls: skimming, taping, compounding, primer coat.
- Complete finish carpentry: casings, moldings, bases, trims.
- Hook up electrical connections.
- Complete final painting.
- Install floor.
- Install cabinets (this sometimes precedes flooring installation).
- Install appliances.
- Hang light fixtures.
- Set countertops.
- Hook up plumbing fixtures.
- Install backsplash.
- Sand and stain wood floors.
- Complete punch list (a detailed list of niggling things to do).
- Celebrate! Break out a bottle of champagne (or ice-cold Diet Coke).

with my design colleagues—architects, contractors, cabinetmakers, plumbers, electricians, contacts at appliance showrooms and marble yards, tile installers—for constructive advice, the kind of advice that is down-to-earth, not pie-in-the-sky.

Most important, I've culled my files and notebooks to collect the best tips and tales from my experience with my own clients, many of whose kitchens you'll see in detail on the upcoming pages. Consider the Mullaneys, who refurbished an old seaside hotel on the Long Island Sound for their large family, and started with no kitchen whatsoever. Compare that to the Marinaccios' urban apartment, which had a decent enough kitchen featuring floor-to-ceiling Formica cabinets that maximized every single inch of coveted city space but were just too antiseptic for them. Raymond Waites's shoe box of a kitchen in East Hampton, New York, was no place for a chef and a showman who needed space and drama. Kristiina Ratia of Connecticut spent decades eating at a table but hungered for an island to hang around as her children entered college and young adulthood. The Chang-Scanlans of Greenwich, Connecticut, wanted it all—their dream kitchen with room to accommodate both large families when they visited. Personally, I just wanted a better-looking, brighter space with access to my beautiful backyard.

Whether you're starting a kitchen from scratch in a new house, renovating a dated one, or simply tweaking a few details here and there to give an already fully functioning space a facelift, the best approach is to think about what's going to work in real life, in the real world, for you and your family. Start from that perspective, and the details—the many, many details—will fall into place.

[ABOVE] HIGH DRAMA: THIS EAST HAMPTON KITCHEN PERFECTLY SUITS THE OWNER, A DESIGNER WITH A FLAIR FOR THE UNEXPECTED AND A PASSIONATE COOK WHO LOVES TO ENTERTAIN.

[LEFT] STRUCTURAL TIE BARS CONCEAL RECESSED LIGHTING SOURCES WHILE ADDING VITAL TEXTURE TO AN ALL-WHITE ROOM. BEAD BOARD, BEAMS, CARERRA MARBLE, AND A WHITE-TILED FLOOR ADD SUBTLE PATTERN TO AN UNDERSTATED YET RICHLY TEXTURED SPACE.

The Big Picture

When it comes to designing a kitchen, many homeowners find getting started the most daunting task of all. You'll be faced with a seemingly endless number of decisions during the project, whether a renovation or brand-new construction. Do you want stone or solid-surface counters? A floor in oak or slate? Recessed lighting or pendants? Chrome or nickel faucets? Knobs or handles? An island, a table, or both? In addition, you must consider the overall configuration and layout of the space itself, which affects not only how the kitchen feels but also how you feel in it. But take heart. A kitchen can be done, and done well. And you don't have to lose your sanity in the process. A lot of people, including me, have been there and back and have advice on how to make the endeavor more manageable.

When and Why to Update

At some point in the life of a kitchen (and its owners), the need for an upgrade will arise. The trigger for change may be small—an oven that finally dies, Formica countertops that are cracking and peeling, or a hopelessly scarred floor. Maybe your cabinet doors no longer close properly and the drawers slide open of their own volition as if poltergeists reside within. Or the trouble might be bigger—too much congestion by the stove, or a dreary space with no view. Or bigger yet: You literally need more space.

The way we live in kitchens has changed dramatically in the past few decades, prompting the need for changes in layout and design. The modern kitchen has evolved into a great room of sorts. More and more, we're blurring the border between a purely functional cook's domain and a true family living space where you can lounge on the sofa, check your e-mail, watch the news, and oversee the kids doing homework.

For a kitchen to be truly modern it should be up to date technologically (with dedicated wiring for gadgets and computers) and ecologically (with a household recycling center, a trash compactor, and a water purifier). Chances are, if your kitchen is older than fifteen years, some element of it is obsolete—most likely the appliances. Most refrigerator manufacturers don't give a warranty longer than twelve years, at which point it makes more sense to buy a new machine than repair the old one. Fridges, stoves, and dishwashers keep getting smarter; this is one area in which replacing appliances when they start to falter is actually a wise investment, as you'll be buying a more efficient model. Just be prepared for the domino effect! Once you replace your old fridge with a sleeker, taller model, for example, not only will your over-fridge cabinet need to be reworked but your other

major appliances will likely look tired by comparison. And you may find yourself craving other kitchen amenities. Along with the big three—fridge, range, and dishwasher—a full-out dream kitchen often includes a prep sink, a beverage center, a wine chiller, and a convection wall oven.

When assembling your wish list of appliances and designing your ideal kitchen—be it a gut renovation or new construction that rises from the ground up in a new house—stay open-minded. Don't lock into one plan, one program, one brand, one theme. Sometimes we are so eager to get going and so determined to finish quickly that we don't allow ourselves the time or the leeway to entertain other ideas. I've been guilty of this kind of tunnel vision before. In our last renovation, I thought I wanted my kitchen doors and adjoining terrace stairs in direct alignment. Well, my yard falls off steeply on that side of the house, and direct alignment would have meant more stairs than the grace-

ful, gradual pair of stairs I ended up with. When the architect broached the subject of staggering the doors and stairs, I was certain the idea was ridiculous. Turned out he was right; my doors and steps don't align, but they direct and guide perfectly.

Everyone talks about how intimidating kitchen design can be, but it can also be exhilarating. It's a genuine thrill to see the project spring from the back-of-the-napkin sketches to the blueprint pages to a three-dimensional working, living, breathing kitchen—the kitchen you dreamed of.

The Key Questions

To formulate a cohesive approach to your kitchen project, you need to pinpoint what you really need and want in the space—how you want it to function, and how *you* want to function in it.

First, think about your cooking style. Are you the sole chef, or do you like to cook with other family members? If the latter, make sure you allow enough counter space to set up more than one cutting board and enough elbow room for side-by-side chopping. Are you a serious baker? If so, you'll probably want a marble surface for dough-rolling and at least one oven with a convection feature. Are you a griller? If you grill a lot, you'll definitely need major ventilation. Do you like to put up soups and sauces? If so, think carefully about your freezer capacity. Do you entertain a lot? Do you need a big table or mega-island as a staging area, two dishwashers, and a double sink? Or are you a take-out family? Would a microwave be more important than a six-burner stove? How critical is speed, for that matter? Do you all sit down together to eat, or do you eat in shifts as family members straggle home? You may want to plan for a warming drawer to keep meals moist and heated for late-comers.

Shopping is next on the strategy list. Let's say you like to buy in bulk—cases of beverages, Dumpster-size cartons of paper towels, and boxes and boxes of cereal. Plan for a pantry space; otherwise, you'll be jamming all that stuff into overflowing cabinets and lamenting the day you didn't think ahead. If you cook a lot of ethnic foods and need a cool, dry spot for a vast array of spices, consider where to place that shelf or cabinet (away from the heat of the stove and south-facing windows). A person who markets daily, stopping in at the fish store, butcher, and greengrocer, won't have the same refrigerator needs as someone who piles a week's worth of groceries in one cart and brings it all home to unload at once.

Then there's the whole question of how the family will use the kitchen in nontraditional ways. Do you envision the children doing homework there? Do you expect to pay bills and write e-mails in the kitchen? Do you see the kitchen as the spot where your kids will

[ABOVE] KITCHEN REDUX: SLIMMER AND SLEEKER MEANS TALLER, TOO. SAY GOOD-BYE TO THE OVER-REFRIGERATOR TRAY CABINET.

[ABOVE] THE ANNEX ADVANTAGE: IT'S CHEAPER, AND OFTEN MORE AESTHETICALLY COHESIVE, TO COLONIZE AN EXISTING STRUCTURE (IN THIS CASE, A PORCH) IN ORDER TO GAIN A FEW CRITICAL FEET IN THE KITCHEN THAN TO BUILD AN ADDITION FROM THE GROUND UP.

[OPPOSITE] ONE OR TWO CUSTOM CABINETRY PIECES CAN BRING PERSONALITY TO THE WHOLE KITCHEN. HERE, A SHALLOW BEAD BOARD-BACKED BOOKSHELF, MADE BY A LOCAL CARPENTER, IS THE PERFECT SPOT FOR COOKBOOKS AND A STRIKING COLLECTION OF POTTERY.

hang out after school, studying or working on art projects or puzzles? Do you want a spot near a window or reading lamp to curl up in and peruse the paper? How about a surface on which to pot plants or cut flowers? You spend so much of your day, night—okay, *life*—in your kitchen that it really pays to customize the space in as many personal ways as possible.

Scouting for Space

After you've defined your broad goals, it's time to think about how you're going to bring them to life in the house you have or are building. Ask yourself if you can fit all of it—the appliances, the storage space, and any new features, such as an island—into the kitchen's footprint. Perhaps you can tweak your current kitchen by reconfiguring cabinets or adding clever interior cabinet storage amenities. If not, now's the time to hunt for neighboring space to appropriate.

Look first at adjacent rooms. In my house, the kitchen backed up to a small laundry room that was barely adequate for my family of six, including two smelly hockey players and two clothes-horse daughters—and not in the right place anyway (the odorous socks and the whir of the washer and dryer were none-too-pleasant company during breakfast and dinner). What I really needed was a bigger laundry room somewhere else and a pantry right by the kitchen. We found the laundry space in a former maid's room on the second floor and retrofitted the old laundry room off the kitchen with storage shelves and hooks for hanging, turning it into a wonderful pantry closet.

Sometimes finding new space is as simple as closing off an overabundance of entries. In one kitchen I saw there were doors leading to the porch, mudroom, family room, front hall, dining room, and basement. No wonder they had no wall space for cabinets: They had no walls! By eliminating several doorways and rerouting traffic, we were able to create a more spacious and sensible kitchen layout.

Another way to create more kitchen space is to steal it—call it creative trespassing. One client of mine dug into the back wall of a built-in china closet in the dining room to grab an extra few feet for her kitchen. I also had a client who broke through into the garage to co-opt more space.

Because the garage sat a few feet lower than the kitchen, she was able to cantilever the new space—that is, hang it like a balcony—over the garage floor. As a bonus, the family got space in the garage, under the cantilevered portion of the kitchen, for storing recyclables. Whenever you can incorporate an existing outlying structure, like a garage or a porch, it will represent a substantial cost savings, as you won't have to do a new roof or foundation.

Looking past the immediate kitchen vicinity for a whole new kitchen location is another creative strategy. If your existing kitchen is poorly located in relation to the rest of the house, think about switching it with another room (not unlike the pantry example above, but on a bigger scale). Clients of mine were looking at a new house. They fell in love with the neighborhood and the property but almost passed on the house because the kitchen was too small, too far from the family room, and had no view to the yard. The dining room, however, was generously sized, with a fireplace and multiple French doors in the back. Once they realized they could switch the two rooms, they were sold.

TRADE TIP

A renovation provides the perfect opportunity to jettison (or donate) the excess and the underused: a long-since-replaced-by-a-Cuisinart blender, warped cookie sheets, old silverware, mismatched glasses, random salad bowls, and the ubiquitous collection of promotional mugs. Going into a new kitchen with just those things you need and truly like is liberating.

[ABOVE] THIS BREAKFAST ROOM BAY CANTILEVERS OFF THE BACK OF THE HOUSE. OFTEN CALLED THE "BUMP IN THE BACK," IT ALLOWS FOR REDUCED CONSTRUCTION COSTS SINCE NO FOUNDATIONAL SUPPORT IS REQUIRED.

TRADE TIP

Cantilevering is basically leveraging, in the truest sense of the word. You can cantilever off an existing structure up to 36 inches without additional foundational supports below. That means no excavating and no additional mechanical upgrades in terms of heat or air.

[LEFT] THE FINAL FLOOR FINISH PHASE TAKES SOME VIGILANCE. DUST PARTICLES IN THE AIR, GENERATED BY SOMETHING AS INNOCENT AS SLAMMING A DOOR, CAN SETTLE (FOREVERMORE) ON THE WET SURFACE. STAY OUT AND BE PRUDENT. LUCKILY, TODAY'S STAINS ARE QUICK DRYING SO THE EXILE WON'T BE LONG.

Another family, with a house on the ocean, decided to turn the library, which faced the water, into the kitchen, and they changed the old, dark kitchen (looking onto the driveway) into a generously sized back pantry.

If you can't work within your existing structure by begging, borrowing, or stealing, you're looking at a bona fide addition. How do you know when it's time to bite the bullet and build? Once you've exhausted the creative possibilities within your existing footprint, it's time to call in the big guns: professional design help (for tips on finding and hiring the pros, see "Survival Guide," page 215). An architect or kitchen designer can see beyond what's there to what can be—specifically speaking, which part of the house to come off of, how best to scale the addition (to the site and to your budget), and how to link the new space, literally and aesthetically, to the existing structure. Will the view be lost or enhanced? What is the best way to capture light? Do you want matching windows? new French doors? a continuing roofline or a pitched gable? How about flow from kitchen to mudroom or out to the backyard? Bottom line, you want the new structure to fit in like a new addition to the family.

Planning and Plotting

A kitchen requires a layout that is defined and designed to a *T* and within a quarter-inch. That explains why kitchen projects should be thought of as a slow cooker. If you want your new kitchen up and running by Thanksgiving, say, then you had better start planning in January. Yes, it takes that long, if not longer. Call it a year.

The main reason planning and executing a kitchen is so time- (and mind-) consuming is that there are so many bits and pieces to account for. A kitchen is the sum of many, many parts, from the obvious big appliances to the smallest details, like hinges and handles. And many of them are permanent, once installed. You'll need to map out the lighting, for example. Once it's up, recessed into the ceiling, surface-mounted in several places, or cut into the backsplash, rejigging the electrical plan is no small endeavor.

Storage, too, takes careful strategy. I find that the best way to calculate how much space you'll need for pots and pans or platters and small appliances is to measure—literally—the spaces your kitchen currently has. If your cast-iron casseroles are crashing up against your nonstick fry pans, or if you have to tip your pasta pot on its side to wriggle it out of a tight spot, you should figure on more storage space in your new cabinet plan. Record the height, width, and depth of all your storage spots and whether they're adequate (in which case you'll want to replicate them) or not (in which case, note why not—too small, awkwardly shaped, etc.). Increasing cabinet sizes by even an inch here or there can make an enormous difference.

Yes, there are countless decisions to make, but don't feel you have to solve every single issue at once. Focus your energy on one distinct area at a time, if possible—the floor plan, the storage, then the cabinets, then the floor—to keep from getting overwhelmed.

[ABOVE] THINK OUTSIDE THE BOX *AND* OUTSIDE THE KITCHEN. TRANSPLANTED TO THE OLD LIBRARY, THIS BEACHSIDE KITCHEN NOW HAS A MESMERIZING VIEW.

TRADE TIP

If you're not really serious (not yet, anyway) about making a purchase, be sensitive about taking too much of a salesperson's time. Let him or her know that you're researching and that you'll be back. Always take a business card; you may need to call with questions, and you'll be able to ask for a particular person by name. If your salesperson is not busy with a ready-to-buy customer, you may get more advice and information than you hoped for.

[ABOVE] GATHER IDEAS AND INSPIRATION. AFTER YOU'VE COLLECTED FAVORITE SAMPLES AND TEAR SHEETS IN AN ENVELOPE OR A BINDER, TRY PINNING THEM UP ON A BOARD (OR PERHAPS A BLANK WALL RIGHT IN THE RENOVATION SPACE) SO THAT YOU CAN SEE HOW YOU AND YOUR FAMILY REACT TO THEM. OVER TIME, THE FRONT-RUNNERS WILL BECOME CLEAR.

[OPPOSITE] IF A SURFACE IS MORE DECORATIVE THAN WORK-ORIENTED (SANS SINK OR CUTTING BOARD), THEN A DELICATE MARBLE MAKES SENSE, SINCE IT WON'T NEED TO BE RESEALED. THIS COUNTERTOP INSPIRED THE HOMEOWNERS TO FAUX-PAINT THE CHINA CABINET TO MATCH.

The Style File

No kitchen is complete without the owner's stamp of style. To establish that vision, first imagine the kind of environment you want to cook and eat in. Are you drawn to the idea of a cozy and comfortable kitchen with soft lighting, or an airy, bright space that's primarily designed for serious cooking? Do you like to see dishes and glassware on display, or do you want yours concealed behind closed cabinet doors?

If you're not sure exactly what you're after, or if you want more direction and inspiration when it comes to the specifics, there's no better resource than photographs in decorating magazines and design books. Start tearing out or marking images you like and collecting them in a folder or a notebook—long before you begin construction, when the new kitchen is still a distant goal. Beyond magazines, think about movie or television kitchens you covet (the well-turned-out kitchen in *Something's Gotta Give* has become something of a touchstone) or friends' kitchens you admire.

Give yourself plenty of time to flip through your idea book. Write notes on Post-its to remind yourself which element in the picture you were drawn to—the stools at the island, the molding around a cabinet door, the color of a range. After a time, you may begin to detect a pattern in your preferences. The images that pop up time and time again are usually a reflection of your true inner decorating voice. Most of us know what we like, deep down; the truth is, we don't really change our decorating stripes all that much. Stylish downtown types usually stay stylish downtown types, even if they move to the suburbs. Homey cooks most often want homey kitchens, and ebullient entertainers always want space for a party. Once you zero in on your kitchen spirit, many of the decisions about colors, appliances, cabinetry, and counters will fall into place.

After weeks or months of musing and mulling, it's time to test your ideas in the real world. Start by window-shopping. Visit kitchen stores and cabinet showrooms. Go to the marble yard. Stop in at the plumbing supply showrooms and appliance stores. Prices vary widely, to say the least. A faucet can cost $140 or $1,350, while a fridge might cost between $800 and, can you believe, $14,000. The more homework you do, the better you'll be able to decide when to splurge and when to scrimp.

By going out into the marketplace you can test, examine, touch, and try things out. What type of cabinets look best to you, and which handle feels good in your hand? Do you like your drawers deep or shallow? What about a spice rack—in a drawer or on the inside of a door? Go to as many showrooms and stores as you have energy for.

[ABOVE] A PENINSULA SEPARATES
CHURCH AND STATE—THE EATING AND
THE LIVING AREAS OF A GENEROUSLY
SIZED KITCHEN—WHILE ALLOWING A
SENSE OF OPENNESS AND FLOW.

[RIGHT] LITTLE DETAILS CAN HAVE
A FAR-REACHING RESULT: A PROPER
PICTURE LIGHT, TYPICALLY SAVED FOR
THE FRONT OF THE HOUSE, ADDS TO
THE OVERALL AMBIENCE DOWN THE
BACK STAIRS AS WELL.

[FAR RIGHT] MORE THAN JUST THE
TYPICAL HORIZONTAL SHELVES: REF-
ERENCES FOR CABINETRY INTERIORS,
THE MORE THE MERRIER, WILL HELP
YOU MAXIMIZE EVERY INCH OF SPACE
AND STORAGE.

Each has its own specialties, and you never know what you'll find. By poking around, I discovered a great pot organizer for a cabinet—one I've since ordered for many clients.

When scoping out appliances, take the time to think about how you'd use them. Swing open a fridge and picture your contents inside. Is there enough room for a platter? All your cartons of juice? Do you think you'll really use that ice crusher in the door, or would you prefer a streamlined front? As for stoves, twist the knobs and reach in as if to take out a roasting pan. You may not want to be doing deep knee bends every evening. Can you picture all your dishes stacked in the dishwasher, or will it be a squeeze?

A trip to the tile store or stone yard to source counters and backsplashes is the next logical step. This can be a treat if, like me, you enjoy the beauty of natural stones and ceramics. Bring along a large canvas bag for giveaway samples (they get heavy) and your camera (so you can take pictures, if allowed, of stones or tiles that aren't available in sample size).

After you've assembled your favorite swatches and samples, lay them out and mock them up in a potential kitchen. Try to place the elements in the right relationship to one another—cabinets vertical, floors and counters horizontal—so you get a good sense of the interplay between shapes, colors, tones, and textures, and, of course, overall style—that is, the big picture.

TRADE TIP

Often, the farther a contractor is located from a major metropolitan area or resort town, the better the pricing. But remember, a long-commute contractor is far afield—not readily available for quick consultations or emergency meetings with a subcontractor. And there's the exhaustion factor—traveling back and forth twice a day may wear on the workers. I've seen plenty of cases where the end-of-the-job details remain unfinished due, simply, to fatigue. For short-term, quick-hit projects, however, this arrangement can work well for everyone.

[ABOVE] CREATING A PERSONAL STYLE IS ALL IN THE DETAILS. HERE, AN INLAID COUNTER AND UNUSUAL HARDWARE MAKE FOR A GLAMOROUS AND UNIQUE ISLAND.

Nailing Down a Budget

There may be no accounting for taste, but you'll certainly have some accounting to do when it comes to your budget. Figuring out the cost of a kitchen is an essential part of bringing the project to life. If you're not realistic from the start about what you can afford to do, you'll end up wasting time—maybe even more money in redrawn plans—and set yourself up for disappointment.

Start with your fully-decked-out wish list, cataloguing every amenity that tempts you. If, as is so often the case (at least *my* case), your eyes are bigger than your budget, it's time to separate the needs from the wants. Everyone has to make trade-offs—it comes with the territory. Which is more important: state-of-the-art appliances or building out a few feet to get more square footage? In the first case, you satisfy the desire for culinary art; in the other, for a generous floor plan.

Because labor is usually the biggest cost factor in a kitchen renovation, it makes sense to understand how contractors structure their bids. I strongly urge you to opt for a fixed bid (which covers the labor of subcontractors as well as the material costs, such as for lumber and Sheetrock) rather than a per-hour bid, also called *time and materials* or *cost-plus.* A time-and-materials bid has no cap; you end up paying for every delay, and the final cost of the job is nearly always higher than going with a fixed bid. As for evaluating initial bids from a few contractors and deciding who has the best price, keep in mind that the cheapest guy is often not the best guy. An inexpensive bid may mean a contractor who cuts corners or rushes the job to get to the next. You might even end up paying more money having to redo mistakes. A stone countertop is, after all, set in stone. You don't want to have to reinstall the counters, let alone replumb or rewire. As important as price is reputation; I would go with a contractor whose work comes highly recommended, especially by a neighbor, a close friend, or a family member who can give you the inside scoop. (For more detailed information on contractors, see "Survival Guide," page 215.)

So where can you shave costs, if not with contractors? With kitchen suppliers. Scrutinize the bid for cabinets, which are typically the second-biggest item in the budget. The best buys in a cabinet showroom are the simplest—an uncomplicated maple or white-painted cabinet. Once you start to add details like raised paneling, carvings, columns, brackets, or glass doors, the costs tick up. Layer in intricate moldings, turned corners, glazed finishes, and interior storage bells and whistles, and the final price may be as much as double that of plainer cabinetry choices. Stone suppliers offer a range of price points, too. Certain commonly quarried stones, such as Crema Marfil, Uba Tuba, Black Absolute, Luna Pearl, and Cashmere Gold, are far less expensive than their exotic counterparts, Blue Bahia, Azul du Mar, and Ivory Gold. And if you opt for a standard edge detailing rather than something more decorative, like a serpentine ogee cut, you will limit the fabrication price. It's also worth asking around about bargains at the marble yard. Sometimes a yard gets stuck with overstock of a stone and may happily sell it at or below cost; one customer's over-order or return may turn into your good deal.

[OPPOSITE] RULES ARE MADE TO BE BROKEN. AN OVERSIZE PIE-SHAPED ISLAND MAY SEEM IDIOSYNCRATIC, BUT NOT WHEN PARTNERED WITH A FREE-HANGING OVEN HOOD—ESPECIALLY WHEN IT IS IN FRONT OF A WINDOW. DON'T BE AFRAID TO THINK OUTSIDE THE BOX.

TRADE TIP

To reduce costs, try to keep the main water, waste, and gas lines where they are. You can replace your fittings, but once you decide to uproot and move them, you incur an additional expense that is sometimes considerable. The exception, of course, is if moving a key line actually makes the kitchen work more efficiently in a new configuration—say, moving the fridge from between the sink and the stove (an awful arrangement) to either end. In that case, the cost may well be worth the change.

TRADE TIP

Your hood will function most effectively if placed 30 inches (for a standard range) to 36 inches (for a pro range) above the cooking surface.

No matter where you cut or sink costs, take solace in the fact that kitchens sell houses. Just ask any Realtor. According to the National Realtor's Association, a kitchen renovation returns a minimum of 80 percent and often 100 percent of the original investment. (In my book, a good kitchen always returns more than 100 percent of its cost in terms of family enjoyment.) To make sure you're at the top end of that resale range, consider these factors:

Will your new kitchen make the rest of the house look shabby? A state-of-the-art kitchen doesn't solve the problem of a former sunroom turned family room that's only 9 feet wide. Make sure there's money left in the budget to address the home's other flaws over time.

- Is the new space compatible with the style of your home inside and out? Your lust for Santa Fe may not cut the mustard in a Mediterranean. A Maine-style cottage kitchen may look at sea in a formal Colonial. While you may love eclecticism, a potential buyer may be put off by the mix.

- Keep it simple. A multilayered, multisurfaced, multi-tiered, multicountered kitchen may reflect every facet of your personality, but some of those facets may be a turn-off to a future buyer.

- Are you just decorating (new cabinets, appliances, surfaces) without fixing the underlying problem (poor flow, no view, limited floor space)? Future owners may well care less about your style and more about how the kitchen works.

- Do you need to add on, or will you be overbuilt on your lot? Even if the zoning board okays an addition, make sure the new space doesn't visually devour the rest of your house or the lot itself.

[RIGHT] IN A BRIGHT, WHITE KITCHEN WITH NO WINDOWS, NATURAL LIGHT ENTERS THROUGH OVERSIZE FRENCH DOORS AND CLEVERLY POSITIONED, GENEROUSLY SCALED SKYLIGHTS. EVERY OUNCE OF DAYLIGHT REFLECTS OFF, AND IS AMPLIFIED BY, THE ALL-WHITE ENVIRONMENT.

- Is yours already the most expensive house on the block? If so, spend carefully so you have some hope of getting a return on your investment.

- If you know you're going to flip a house, say, as soon as the kids start school, you'll likely want to spend more on those things that attract the average buyer (like a stone countertop) than cater to your own personal needs.

- If this is an interim house rather than your forever home, think twice before going all out on fanciful amenities such as pasta spigots or falling water faucets, which may look tired before you get to market.

- Decide on your kitchen star—floor, walls, or counters—and let the rest of the setting be a tasteful backdrop. Yes, you should invest in good quality (appliances and materials) where possible, setting a base standard for the space. But don't indulge in every piece or detail of the kitchen, or you'll go over the top—and over budget.

[LEFT] THE SLIMMEST OF DO-IT-YOURSELF SHELVING PROVIDES ADDITIONAL LINEAR FEET OF STORAGE AND MILES OF STYLE. EXISTING WHITE-TILED WALLS WERE LEFT INTACT, CREATING A WARM BACKDROP FOR HIGH-TECH SHELVING.

The Layout

Good kitchen design always starts with the layout. Determining how all the elements—the appliances, counters, tables, and chairs—stack up and sort out is paramount to making a kitchen work smoothly, efficiently, and artfully. That's why a floor plan requires a well-thought-out overall plan, one that takes into account that the kitchen has grown dramatically in scope, not to mention sheer square footage.

Simply put, there are more decisions to make now about what goes where. We're far beyond the days when you needed only to decide where to plug in the fridge or plunk down the stove. The kitchen is no longer the utility room at the back of the house, with small windows and the most basic architecture, a room solely for cooking and eating. My childhood kitchen memories are of scraping dishes and making toast. I never remember anyone other than immediate family being in the kitchen, or doing anything in the room that didn't revolve around food.

Fast-forward a few decades, and the kitchen has been elevated to prime status. It's the new hub—almost like the "everything room" of colonial times, in which the home's activities centered on the main hearth. One could say the kitchen is back where it started: front and center. It has become the place to sort mail and school schedules, recycle bottles, carve pumpkins, cut flowers, groom the dog, read the paper, watch the news, check e-mail, and, last but not least, entertain. We're even throwing parties in the kitchen! Just about the only thing we don't do there these days is sleep. My father-in-law used to say that we can now live in the kitchen and rent out the rest of the house.

With the kitchen's expanded role comes a host of new items to work into the space. A typical kitchen has cabinets of different sizes, an island or a table, appliances both major and auxiliary, and a wide spectrum of lighting fixtures. You have to fit it all in, the accoutrements and the activities, and still have room to move about. Kitchens are alive with movement—comings and goings, fixings and food.

As kitchens have become more significant, they've also become more stylish. No longer is it unusual to see glass doors and chandeliers. In my own kitchen, I've added a wall of glass in the form of not one but three sets of French doors that lead out to the terrace and backyard. It's the best view in the house.

[OPPOSITE] OFTEN LIGHT, AIR, AND BREATHING SPACE ARE JUST AS IMPORTANT AS THE DISTANCE BETWEEN YOUR SINK AND STOVE. DON'T GET HUNG UP ON THE OUTDATED WORK TRIANGLE.

Coming Up with a Plan

Whether you're creating a kitchen from scratch or renovating an existing space, the key to getting what you want is *knowing* what you want. It sounds obvious, but if you take the time to ask yourself the pertinent questions about how you'll work and live in the kitchen, you'll end up with a clear vision for a floor plan—one that's tailor-made for you, your family, and the space itself. Think about your kitchen from a personal point of view. You don't want to get locked into a generic or stock idea of how a kitchen is supposed to be laid out; that will only limit the possibilities for your ideal kitchen.

Start configuring the space by doing a walk-through—mentally or literally—of a typical day, factoring in the usual activities and the usual cast of characters (people and pets). Be an actor. Pretend you're coming in the back door with arms full of groceries. Is there a surface nearby on which to put down the bags and the keys? Then imagine getting a meal ready. Walk from the fridge to the sink and back; pull out a pot; grab your cookbooks; set the table; load and unload the dishwasher. Think, too, about relaxing in the space. Where are you going to put a comfortable chair in which to read the paper? How about a sunny spot for morning coffee? You'll want a layout where getting a second cup doesn't require circling the entire kitchen or tripping over the dog bed. Make sure there's room in the scenario for friends and family as well. Do you and the supporting cast members have room to navigate past and around one another?

While you're going through the motions of an average day, don't forget to consider what it's like to see the kitchen from other rooms. Peer at the space through various portals—of the dining room, study, terrace, foyer—and picture the view along various sight lines. Most kitchens are on display from several perspectives through open doorways or doors that are never closed. Who wants the first image to be a sink loaded with dishes? How much cleaner, more chic, to glimpse a stainless-steel hood or a win-

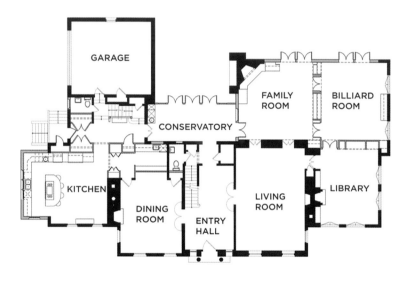

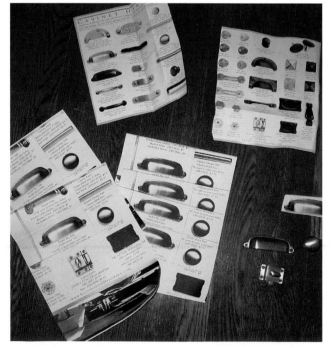

[ABOVE] A SMALL BUMP-OUT (AT LEFT), A MERE 6-FOOT EXPANSION, CREATES ENOUGH NEW SPACE IN THIS PLAN TO ALLOW FOR BOTH AN ISLAND AND A TABLE.

[LEFT] A CABINET'S FUNCTION AND WHAT YOU CHOOSE TO STORE INSIDE IT DETERMINES, IN PART, WHAT KIND OF HARDWARE TO USE. HEAVY-DUTY DRAWERS NEED A GOOD, STURDY HANDLE. BIN PULLS ARE BEST FOR CUTLERY AND SMALLER DRAWERS.

[OPPOSITE] AN ALMOST INVISIBLE COOKTOP CONTRIBUTES TO THE CLEAN, COOL LOOK OF THIS PRISTINE KITCHEN. POSITIONING A COOKTOP IN FRONT OF A WINDOW MIGHT SEEM LIKE AN ODD CHOICE. BUT A 4-INCH BACKSPLASH KEEPS THE FIX-INS FROM, WELL, SPLASHING, ONTO THE WINDOWSILL BEHIND.

[ABOVE] LETTING IN THE LIGHT: A GLASS DOOR AND WALL-TO-WALL WINDOWS IN THIS BREAKFAST AREA FEATURE OVERSIZE PANES (SMALL PANES TEND TO COMPROMISE THE VIEW BY CLUTTERING IT UP WITH WOOD MULLIONS).

[RIGHT] MATTE (OR HONED) BLACK GRANITE MIMICS SOAPSTONE AND PARTNERS BEAUTIFULLY WITH A STAINLESS-STEEL DISHWASHER, THE HANDLE OF WHICH DOUBLES AS A TOWEL RACK.

dow over a breakfast table. Think in terms of composition, using the frame of a door as a viewfinder. The more complete the image (the center of the stove rather than just a corner, for instance), the more pleasing to the eye.

As long as you're in the land of What If, fast-forward and imagine how your kitchen is likely to be used five or ten years from now. Will your family be growing? Young parents often don't think about where their children will eventually spread out and do homework. And parents of tweens and teens don't always consider how the kitchen's usage will change once the nest begins emptying. In our home, the breakfast room is becoming my husband's and my primary TV-watching area. Only when the kids are home from college do we venture into the more traditional family room. Then, for a brief time, the kitchen reverts to its full-fledged purpose and plan.

Putting Thoughts to Paper

If your kitchen is a renovation of an existing space, you can use your current floor plan as a template for the new; it helps to have something to work from. Measure the room, including all fixed features such as windows, doors, and ceiling heights. (You don't need to be detailed; believe me, the contractor or cabinet fabricator will verify all measurements.) Next, note the location of the appliances—be aware that moving an appliance often means moving the plumbing or gas line that feeds

TRADE TIP

Once you get a sketch of the existing floor plan down (generated by you, your architect, or a computer program), it's easy to experiment with layout scenarios by using pieces of tracing paper. Simply place the paper on top of the sketch and go to town: Add a sink here or a warming drawer there, realign a door or a fridge, or draw in French doors. In the process, you might discover a glitch in the plan. The path from the back door to the fridge, for instance, might require a tricky navigation of the island. By noodling around on tracing paper, you can identify and fix mistakes. And if your ideas look good on paper, they're more likely to look good in reality.

[ABOVE] KEEP PERSPECTIVE IN MIND: AN OPEN EXPANSE FROM THE DINING ROOM TO THE KITCHEN TO THE FRENCH DOORS BEYOND CREATES A STRONG, LONG SIGHT LINE, ESPECIALLY IN A SMALL SPACE.

A QUICK KITCHEN CHECKLIST: WHAT YOU'VE GOT AND WHAT YOU WANT

Flaws in the Current Plan

Part of cooking up a new kitchen is pinpointing what doesn't work in your current one—from the biggest to the smallest annoyances. Here's an example of one client's list. Food for thought!

STORAGE

- Not enough cabinets to accommodate dishes and glassware
- No room for bulk items, such as paper towels and dog food
- A too-small coat closet/mudroom
- No pantry at all

APPLIANCES

- Fridge juts into the room
- One oven not enough
- Dishwasher sits too far from the dish storage

LIGHTING

- Not enough lighting over the work area
- Too few windows
- Shadows cast by poorly placed recessed light sources

COUNTERS

- Not enough countertop by the sink for prepping
- No surface near the door for keys and groceries
- No island for cooking or hanging out

SEATING

- No table to gather around as a family
- Not enough space for kids to do homework or art projects
- No comfortable spot to read the paper

TRAFFIC FLOW

- Kids get in the way of the cook
- Chairs at the table block access to the back door
- Distance too long between the sink and the cooktop

Fixes for the New Plan

Once you've flagged the kitchen's flaws, it's time to start imagining what you want to add or make room for in your new design. List all your wishes, whether you think you can afford them or not. Otherwise, there might not be room (in the space or your budget) to layer them in later on.

- Computer station or message center
- File storage
- Homework area
- Double sink or second sink
- Entertaining space
- Larger mudroom
- Play area for little kids
- Family-centered cooking space
- Secondary appliances: compactor, cappuccino maker, food processor, rice cooker, water purifier, wine chiller, warming drawers, a second wall oven

it, a potentially expensive proposition. Factor in traffic patterns, and while you're at it, snap some pictures, especially of unusual features or limitations. The photos can help a cabinet-maker or a contractor figure out how to work around that odd window or awkward entrance.

In the process of drawing up a floor plan, don't omit the outside. During the preliminary planning phase of designing a new or renovated kitchen, consider access and views to the outdoors. In fact, bringing a bit of the outside in—by opening up walls and adding windows or doors—is one of the major inspirations for homeowners to renovate. Certainly that was the case for me and my family when we moved into an 85-year-old Colonial that had only a few small windows in the kitchen. It had been remodeled, or remuddled, in the 1970s. The original interior walls of the kitchen—a patchwork of spaces, including a cold storage room

and a staff dining room (yes, that's how it was labeled on the original floor plans)—had been taken down to make one ample kitchen-breakfast room. But the exterior shell was left intact, with a pair of small double-hung windows that were impossible to open and a single side door that deposited family and friends into the driveway by the garbage bins. As a result, the kitchen felt cut off from the backyard just beyond its walls. By swapping the windows for a series of French doors, we created a more gracious and practical entry to the house—and a glorious view from the kitchen.

[TOP] COUNTER INTELLIGENCE: IF YOU HAVE THE ROOM, IT MAKES CULINARY SENSE TO ADD A LOWER-HEIGHT SECONDARY COUNTER, IDEAL FOR ROLLING OUT PASTRY DOUGH OR PROVIDING A PLACE FOR KIDS TO PLAY SOUS-CHEF.

[ABOVE] THIS ADDITION LOOKS OF A PIECE WITH THE COUNTER, AND HELP-FULLY PROVIDES SPACE FOR DINING.

[LEFT] A KITCHEN IS MADE UP OF MANY SURFACES. STONE HAS POLISH, STAINLESS STEEL HAS SHEEN, AND CERAMICS ARE REFLECTIVE. WITH ALL THOSE SHINY SURFACES, A MATTE FINISH CABINET IS A BETTER CHOICE.

[OPPOSITE] A SECONDARY KITCHEN GETS TO SKIP A LOT OF THE HARD WORK AND HAVE SOME FUN. MICROWAVE-FRIENDLY (IT'S HIDDEN UNDER THE COUNTER) WITH NARY AN OVEN OR COOKTOP IN SIGHT, ITS OPEN SHELVING, STAINLESS STEEL, AND EBONY-STAINED ALDER WOOD ARE SEASONED WITH A DASH OF PAPRIKA.

[ABOVE] AN OVERSIZE ISLAND SERVES AS THE COUNTERPOINT TO A STRAIGHT LINEUP OF APPLIANCES, CREATING A TRIANGLE OF SORTS.

The New Kitchen Geometry

The conventional wisdom that you should arrange the three major appliances (fridge, sink, and stove) in a triangular relationship—is, well, conventional. The original concept, developed by researchers at Cornell University in the 1950s, dictated no less than 12 and no more than 22 feet between the three principal points. The formula was meant to reduce the number of steps you have to take while preparing a meal—and it worked because the kitchen was for nothing but cooking, cleaning, and eating. These days, however, kitchens tend to be multitasking, larger spaces, with islands and peninsulas dotting the landscape. The old geometric formula doesn't always apply.

Instead, I like to think outside the triangle and in terms of zones: food preparation zones, food consumption zones, and cleanup zones. The zones, or distinct areas, should coexist without butting up against one another. For example, you'll want the fridge to be far enough away from the cooking zone that the kids won't have to pass right by the hot stove on their way to get a snack. To cut down on congestion, you'll want that frequent pit stop, the beverage center, located on the periphery of the kitchen, far from the sink. Zones are a useful way to think of accommodating auxiliary appliances you might want to work in, such as dishwasher drawers, wall ovens, microwaves, wine refrigerators, and cappuccino centers.

To lay out a kitchen with all these zones, it helps to think more like an urban planner than a mathematician. Much of the placement comes down to traffic flow. In my kitchen, for example, there's the route from the back stairs through the breakfast room to the kitchen island with its cooktop, a trajectory from the sink to the pantry, and a

[ABOVE] TRADITIONALLY, A DISH-WASHER IS PLACED TO THE LEFT OF THE SINK, BUT SOMETIMES RULES ARE MEANT TO BE BROKEN. HERE, TO AVOID CROWDING THE STOVE AND THE PREP AREA, THE DISHWASHER WAS PLACED TO THE RIGHT—WHICH WORKED OUT NICELY FOR THE LEFT-HANDED OWNERS.

line from the sink through the French doors to the terrace. Well, you get the picture—I mean path. It's all been ergonomically planned so no one's bumping into anyone and the appliances have plenty of breathing room.

Placing the Main Elements

A kitchen layout works best when the workhorses, the major appliances, are situated to make cooking and cleaning—that is, life—easier.

The sink is the single most important element to locate. From a size standpoint, the sink and its neighboring counter space, as well as the base cabinet it sits in—often the largest in the kitchen—take up a lot of real estate. From a usage standpoint, the sink soaks up a lot of time. You spend more than 30 percent of your total kitchen time at the sink—prepping food, using the disposal or compactor, washing and drying dishes. So where a sink lives really matters. This point may seem obvious: If possible, place your sink under a window. If that just doesn't work and you must situate your sink against a wall, consider downsizing the upper cabinets lest you feel claustrophobic or actually bop your head. Rather than installing standard-height upper cabinets, opt for shorter or shallower ones, or eliminate them altogether and install 6-inch-deep open shelves—ideal for cups and glasses.

If the sink-at-the-window scenario doesn't fall into place and the upper cabinets are simply too boring a vista to contemplate, there's always the option of dropping a sink into an island. This way, if you can't look outside, you can at least look out over the room. The main drawback of the island site is the attendant mess or spread. Think of the drying rack you'll have to look at day in and day out, not to mention the clutter of bottles, sponges, scrubbers, and soap dispensers on display (a soap dispenser against a perpendicular wall is insignificant; in the open air, it's an eyesore!). Simply put, an island sink is for neatniks only.

Once you've situated the sink, decide where to put the dishwasher. Industry wisdom has it that if you're right-handed, you want your dishwasher on the left, and vice versa. Frankly, unloading and loading the dishwasher does not require the fine motor skills of a dominant hand (and anyway, using your clumsier secondary hand is said to increase brain power and acuity). It's more important to put the dishwasher on the side closer to the cabinets in which you'll be

FIELD NOTE

Odd as it sounds, when Beth and Kevin Mullaney bought the Belvedere, a grand Victorian hotel converted into a home for the aged, they were initially uncertain about where to locate the family kitchen. The original kitchen was condemned, along with a fair amount of the rest of the building. As the couple paced and pondered the remaining house with their four kids (ages from preschool to high school), they found themselves drawn again and again to a three-story turret facing the Long Island Sound. The stunning view was enticing enough on the first floor but even better on the second, which was eye level with the blue water.

In a bold move, the Mullaneys decided to build the kitchen in the turret on the second level, where they could take advantage of the view and the wide and gracious wraparound porch, one floor up and removed from the street. As for the practicality of a second-floor kitchen, there was no need to worry. The original elevator (doesn't every hotel have one?) still worked, which meant no schlepping up the groceries.

Building a kitchen in the round had its challenges. Major decisions, especially regarding storage, were dictated by the views, which the Mullaneys wanted to preserve unobstructed. This meant no upper cabinets. At all. Not only were the Mullaneys limited by the windows (nothing to complain about, mind you), but the geometry of the room constrained them as well. How would they fit everything a big family needed—for cooking, eating, hanging out—into one rather small, oddly shaped space?

Positioning the refrigerator was relatively straightforward. A flat wall that extended from within to just outside the turret provided the logical spot for a built-in refrigerator/freezer. It was adjacent to the family room, so the kids could get snacks without invading the cooking area. But with so many windows and so few walls, where to install the range? In this case, the winning choice was unexpected. The Mullaneys placed the full-size commercial Viking range and hood in front of one of the windows facing a side street. This allowed them to situate the sink and the dishwasher under the window with the prime water view.

The final and trickiest piece of the puzzle was designing the ideal island for the circular space. The solution was an oversized pie wedge that anchors the center of the room without crowding the space visually and provides plenty of storage for tableware, pots and pans, and glasses, along with recycling bins and that convenient amenity, the warming drawer. The island, like the rest of the layout, honors the quirkiness of the old house but makes it work for a thoroughly modern family.

[ABOVE LEFT] THE BIGGER THE SINK, THE BIGGER THE UNDER CABINET, WHICH CAN MEAN A LOT OF WASTED SPACE, EVEN AFTER YOU'VE ADDED IN AMENITIES LIKE AN INSTANT HOT WATER TAP OR A GARBAGE DISPOSAL. HOME STORES ARE STOCKED WITH ALL SORTS OF NEW SPACE-SAVING ORGANIZERS, SUCH AS THIS TWO-TIERED PULLOUT WIRE RACK.

[ABOVE RIGHT] DISH DETAIL: A SLEEKER ALTERNATIVE TO THE UBIQUITOUS AND UNSIGHTLY DISH DRAIN THAT SITS OUT ON THE COUNTER 24/7.

[OPPOSITE] AD-HOC LANDING SPOT: WITH A WALL OVEN YOU HAVE TO CONSIDER WHERE YOU'LL SET A HOT POT WHEN YOU PULL IT OUT. IN A KITCHEN WITH NO NEARBY COUNTER SPACE, YOU HAVE TO GET CREATIVE. THIS COOK HAS STRATEGICALLY POSITIONED A VINTAGE METAL STOOL AS A HEAT-RESISTANT SURFACE.

storing the dishware. For me, a rightie, that means on the right. If I subscribed to the old advice and put it on the left, I'd have to triple my steps to get to the cabinet.

Placement of the cooktop or range is the next priority. It makes sense to position the burners fairly close to the sink, since the cooktop and the sink are in a symbiotic relationship. Who wants to lug dirty pans all the way across the room to soak, or carry pots of boiling pasta water back to the sink to drain? Even if you spring for a pasta spigot over the stove, you'll still need to transport the heavy pot to the sink to drain the spaghetti. The relationship works the other way, too. You want to be able to chop food at the sink and easily transfer it to a sauté pan on the cooktop. At the same time, however, you don't want the sink and the cooktop *so* close you risk bumping into the sous-chef at the sink.

Sometimes a logical setting for the cooktop is right in the middle of the island—and the action. This allows the cook to carry on a conversation while stirring or whisking without turning his or her back to the room. In my view, an island is not an ideal spot for a sink (which is used countless times a day), but it does make a good home for a cooktop (which is usually used daily, but less often). An island cooktop does, however, raise venting questions. There are two basic solutions: an overhanging hood, which adds drama but cuts view and light; or a downdrafted venting system, which hides the mechanism under the counter, creating a clean look but a less powerful draw than the standard, visible overhanging hood. You could also opt for neither and throw open the windows. That's what we do in our kitchen, with its island cooktop. Fortunately, we have plenty of windows and doors, so onions and other strong odors waft right out.

Wall ovens allow a little more latitude in terms of placement than do sinks or cooktops. Prime reason: Ovens are used far less often than the other basic appliances. After all, you

THE SPACE BETWEEN

Positioning all the elements in a kitchen is only part of the layout equation. Determining the number of inches to leave between them—the clearances—is just as important. How much room to allow between a sink and an island? a fridge and a dishwasher door? a back door and a back stair? Certain minimum clearances are needed to open cabinet doors, warming drawers, and the like to avoid clashes of dishes or bodies.

People, too, need room to maneuver comfortably without banging into corners of doors or handles of appliances. As a cook, you're often moving at warp speed and brandishing sharp knives or hot pots. Ideally, you want the fast lanes (from sink to stove and from stove to table) to be free and clear of traffic.

Just bear in mind that guidelines are only a guide. For years, my family's kitchen table sat only 22 inches from the wall—dramatically closer than the 36 inches any sane kitchen designer would recommend. Still, it allowed us to have a large table in the space, and I could still manage to squeeze behind my kids in their chairs, albeit while sucking in my stomach and standing on tiptoe. Of course, you'd want a little more breathing room if you could get it!

Here are a few guidelines to get you started—then fudge if you will, when you will.

- **BETWEEN COUNTER AND ISLAND.** If this particular aisle is being used as a main thoroughfare into or out of the kitchen, you need a wide berth—roughly 60 inches. But if the space is a work zone with appliances on both sides—a sink on one side and a cooktop on the other, say—you need to allow just 48 inches or so. If appliances line only one side, then 40 inches, even 37, if pressed, is sufficient.

- **AROUND THE SINK.** Allow at least 24 inches on one side of the sink for stacking and drying; that's a logical dimension, given that the sink's frequent companion, the dishwasher, is 24 inches wide. If possible, flank the other side of the sink with a matching 24 inches or more. A 36-inch stretch of counter space is ideal for prepping and for piling up plates and pots after a party.

- **AROUND THE STOVE.** Make sure there is room on the counter—between 18 and 24 inches—near the range or wall oven to create a landing and loading spot for hot and heavy pots. At least one of the nearby surfaces should be heat resistant so you can set down a steaming roasting pan or cookie sheet without worry. Also, allocate about 48 inches between the cooktop and the sink—a comfortable working distance.

- **AROUND THE FRIDGE.** Situate the fridge at least 36 inches away from the sink so these two major elements each have room to breathe. Be sure your plan includes a span of countertop close at hand—ideally, a bare minimum of 18 inches of counter right next to the fridge for loading and unloading foodstuff. The run of counter that sits between the sink and the fridge tends to be the prime meal preparation zone, so keep it clear of appliance garages and armoire-style to-the-counter cabinets that compromise countertop surface.

- **AROUND THE ROOM'S CORNERS.** In areas where countertop appliances meet up with a tall appliance, be it a refrigerator or a wall oven, allow about 16 inches between the appliance and the vertical element to avoid bumping your elbows each time you use the appliance.

- **AROUND THE UPPER CABINETS.** The ideal height to hang upper cabinets is 16 to 18 inches above the countertops. Anything shorter, and you shadow the countertop; anything taller, and the cabinets become less accessible.

[ABOVE] IN A CITY KITCHEN TIGHT ON SPACE, YOU CAN GET AWAY WITH THE MINIMAL DISTANCE (39 INCHES) RATHER THAN THE STANDARD (48 INCHES) BETWEEN THE CABINETS AND THE PENINSULA.

[RIGHT] THIS GENEROUS ISLAND ANCHORS THE KITCHEN AND OFFERS PLENTY OF PREMIUM SPACE FOR MEAL PREP AND DINING.

put something in, take something out, baste, or peek through the window—that's the bulk of it. Wall ovens should be placed at the end of a run of cabinetry, not interrupting it and the countertop. Otherwise, you create a great divide every time you try to shift from counter surface to counter surface. It is critical that you leave some counter space on one side of the oven so you've got a spot to put a hot pot down. Another temperature tip: Don't place the oven right next to the fridge. They're opposites (one hot, one cold) and shouldn't be working against each other.

As for locating the refrigerator itself, think in terms of easy access. This appliance, more than any other, is family territory—open to everyone, seemingly much of the time! Between kids and adults poking around, pulling stuff out, or simply standing there gaping, it gets used by all. As a rule of thumb, you want to place the fridge away from the main food prep area, especially the sink; a distance of 48 inches is a generous minimum. (In my previous home, I had a jam-packed 24 inches. My current 72 inches is bountiful.) Given the choice, it's nice to have the fridge in striking distance of the kitchen table. You don't want to have to walk halfway across the room to refill a glass of orange juice. If that's not feasible, consider installing a refrigerator drawer or two in a convenient spot. Such a drawer, albeit pricy, can slip unobtrusively into a layout, sliding under almost any part of the counter.

Another consideration is the coolness factor. Because the fridge is designed for food storage, it's best not to place it on an interior wall between two rooms. A refrigerator will run more efficiently on an exterior wall, preferably a north-facing wall and not a south-facing wall (or in the path of a south-facing window), where the sun will beat down on it half the day.

The direction of the door swing matters, too. If you're positioning the fridge flush into a corner of the kitchen, at the end of a run of cabinets—a typical spot—be sure to allocate room for the full swing of the door, including the handle. If you can only open the door ninety degrees, you won't be able to pull the storage bins all the way out—a daily irritation—making thorough cleaning a near impossibility. Still, should you find your plan is in a jam, keep in mind that it's often possible to have the fridge's door rehung so it swings out, and swings freely, the opposite way.

The Island

The island has contributed, more than any other kitchen innovation, to creating a social environment in what was once primarily a work space. Yes, islands are first and foremost practical; they offer a generous chopping/slicing/mixing surface and can house sinks, warming drawers, and beverage centers. But they also have less tangible assets. An island is a place to gather around casually, talk with the cook, or read the paper with morning coffee. It can also act as a physical buffer in the space, diverting foot traffic away from heavy-use areas, like a sink or a stove, or blocking the clutter of the vestigial work area from view. One could say that the island—be it big, small, or peninsula—has become almost a fourth family member of the kitchen, along with the three major appliances.

When fitting an island into your plan, think about a real island with water (in this case, floor space) on all sides. You want to have plenty of room to navigate—a 360-degree flow. The basic rule is a minimum of 36 inches of walk-by space in each direction to avoid interference with an appliance (other than the big three), cabinet, or table while seated at the island.

If there's simply no room for an island, don't give up on the concept altogether. Consider a peninsula, which is anchored to the flanking cabinetry so it's open on three sides. One Manhattan-based client of mine tethered a peninsula with a sink to a side wall that had a shallow bank of cabinets under loft-size windows. Had he opted for a free-floating island, it would have intruded into his open entry area. Another city client installed an eating peninsula in her apartment kitchen, cleverly attaching it to a utility column that runs the building's HVAC.

Besides merely fitting into a floor plan, an island should be comfortably sized—not oversized. If you can't reach across the expanse to pass a plate, the island is probably too wide. I find the ideal width is 38 to 42 inches; more than 4 feet and it's a stretch, literally. If you plan to have seating on one side, the overhang factors into the overall measurement. Remember, most of the width is already taken up by the standard depth base storage cabinets

[RIGHT] THE BEAUTY OF AN ISLAND: IT ALLOWS FOR CONVERSATION WITH COMPANY BUT KEEPS THE COOK'S MESS ON THE SINK SIDE.

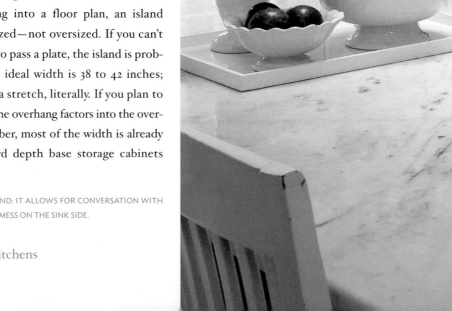

TRADE TIP

While 12 to 15 inches is an ideal overhang for a countertop—roomy enough to slip stools all the way under—if your space is constrained, you can get away with a smaller projection. In a pinch, I've even done 8 inches, give or take—and I'll take it, if the choice is between a slightly confined ledge and no island seating at all.

below (about 2 feet), which leaves an overhang of 1 foot or more—just enough for stools and legs.

An island can adapt to almost any kitchen and any style. It can be short and square, long and linear, pie-shaped, or oval. It can be single- or multilevel, with an eating section elevated from counter height (36 inches) to bar height (42 inches). An island comes with or without seating. You can coordinate the island with the overall cabinetry or treat it as a freestanding piece of furniture. It can be clad in simple bead board or dressed for fine dining with inlaid woods.

Whatever its design, an island is an effective way to separate church and state, so to speak. Like a low partition, it helps differentiate the zones of the kitchen, which can make the room feel more organized and lend a certain area—like the breakfast table—its own room-within-a-room quality. You can also strategically block unsightly sight lines with an island. Let's say the view from your front hall runs straight to the sink. An island interrupts that path and vastly improves the view upon entering. In some cases, it makes sense to add a second "story"—a shallow raised shelf of 6 to 10 inches—to the island's countertop, creating a tall visual screen in the foreground that shields not only a sink's dishes but also any clutter or piles of papers on the surface of the island itself. This type of variable-height, or bilevel, island is not as streamlined, sleek, and, let's face it, stylish as a single-level island, but it's not a bad solution in a busy (code for messy) kitchen.

Not only can the island serve as a buffer but it also can serve as a buffet. For small dinner parties, my husband and I invite our guests to join us in the kitchen while we're getting dinner ready to serve in the dining room. We set the wine and hors d'oeuvres out on the island (instead of gathering in the living room around a cocktail table) and let everyone help themselves. It's a social, relaxed way to start the evening.

[BELOW] PENINSULAS HAVE ONLY ONE POINT OF ENTRY. ESSENTIALLY A DEAD END, A PENINSULA CONSERVES FLOOR SPACE BUT RESTRICTS TRAFFIC FLOW.

TRADE TIP

Ergonomically speaking, your prime storage space is between 30 and 60 inches high. In cabinet terms, that translates into the space from your base cabinet cutlery drawer to the first and second shelves of an upper cabinet. The maximum easily reached storage height is 72 inches—any higher and you'll need a stepstool. Keep in mind that you can't peer into the contents of any drawer that sits over 56 inches above the floor without a stepladder either.

TRADE TIP

Pulling a stool up to an island requires knee room. While 12 to 15 inches is ideal, even a shallow overhang is fine for kids and quick meals.

[ABOVE] TAKE ADVANTAGE OF VERTICAL SPACE. A SMARTLY DE-SIGNED PANTRY KEEPS HEIGHT IN MIND. A DRAWER SHOULD BE NO TALLER THAN EYE LEVEL, SO YOU CAN PEER IN AT THE CONTENTS. OPEN SHELVES FROM THERE ON UP ARE THE BEST STRATEGY.

On the Periphery

The big three appliances drive much of a kitchen's layout, but what of the auxiliary or ancillary appliances—where do they fit in? Even the most seasoned kitchen planners have limited experience placing these secondary players. After all, who even heard of dishwasher drawers a few years ago? That said, here are several guidelines that depend on both a good eye and a strong sense of kitchen design.

Double Dishwashers.
If you're going to have two, make sure one is clearly—visibly—dominant and the other just as clearly designated for the overflow from dinners and parties (discreetly located in the island, for instance). To do that, keep some distance between them. While your inclination may be to flank a sink with a pair of dishwashers, it actually makes more sense to place the units farther from each other. Otherwise, you end up putting dishes willy-nilly in both, only to spend unnecessary time transferring dishes from one to another to get a full load going. One client has gone so far as to put a latch on the secondary unit to stop family members from unintentional loading.

Warming Drawers.
The name *drawer* makes them sound diminutive, but these warming appliances are actually quite hefty—a good 27 or 30 inches wide, with handles that project a full 3 inches. Not only do you need to find a spot that is wide and deep enough, you also want to avoid situating a warming drawer opposite another appliance to avoid the dueling doors dilemma. A pulled-out warming drawer and a flopped-open dishwasher door could cause a real logjam. A smart spot for a warming drawer is in a vertical stack along with a wall oven or two.

Beverage Centers.
These are just begging to be near the table or island—wherever the family gathers or snackers pass on their way in and out the door. By the same token, you want the beverage center as far away as possible from the hurly-burly of the sink, dishwasher, cooktop, and refrigerator. You don't want someone studying drink options while you're trying to unload the dishwasher or get dinner going.

Wine Chillers.
These status symbols deserve their own station, if possible. Whether undercounter or freestanding, wine chillers often look most at home when flanked by furniture-like cabinetry. In terms of placement, position a wine center where it is accessible to guests and not in the heart of the cooking zone. Remember, too, that wine coolers are great for keeping party hors d'oeuvres and cheeses at just the right temperature and ready to serve.

TRADE TIP

Sometimes a trade-off is necessary to squeeze everything you want in the kitchen into one space. One family of five could allow only 37 inches between their island and the sink; also, a warming drawer in the island projected out, making the dimension feel even more cramped. Still, they decided they'd rather live with a bit of a bottleneck in that spot than give up any surface area on their island.

[OPPOSITE] A MANUFACTURER-PROVIDED "TRIM KIT" GIVES YOUR MICROWAVE A SLEEK BUILT-IN LOOK WHILE PROVIDING ADEQUATE VENTILATION FOR AIR AND HEAT CIRCULATION.

A PANTRY CABINET, ORIGINAL TO ANOTHER HOUSE, BALANCES THE FRIDGE AT THE OPPOSITE END OF A BANK OF SEMI-CUSTOM CABINETS. WONDERFUL STORAGE, PLATE-LOADS OF CHARM.

Table Talk

Like an island, a kitchen table accommodates people, facilitates conversation, and serves as a gathering spot—but the two are very different entities. The island is designed more for hanging out and quick meals. People often stand around or lean on an island, like a bar. If you have enough room for a kitchen table as well, go for it; there's simply no substitute. At a table, you sit for longer periods and longer meals in real chairs rather than perched on a stool at an island. A table encourages lingering and conversation. It's the place where kids can spread out with school projects, where you can sort mail or check your laptop. Some homeowners, pressed to choose between table and island, might opt for the table—for example, when the kitchen would feel too cramped or chopped up by an island (or even a peninsula). In some scenarios, a table, small and round or long and narrow, simply fits more naturally and gracefully into the space.

In locating a table, the first consideration, of course, is where there's enough room. A table requires at least a 3-foot radius around the perimeter to allow for chairs to be scooted out. If at all possible, take advantage of natural light and any views to the outside. When you're starting your renovation or construction plan, you might even consider adding more windows or enlarging those that exist in order to make an eat-in table more inviting. One client in Atlanta replaced small windows set high in the wall over the breakfast table with a bank of larger and lower windows, capturing not only more light but a beautiful and unexpected view of the backyard. When the family sat at the table, they were treated to an eye-level expanse of green that was far more enchanting than the sliver of sky glimpsed through the former windows.

[TOP] BRINGING NEW LIFE TO AN OLD KITCHEN. AN OVERSIZE ISLAND AND OVERSCALE WINDOWS FRESHEN UP A TRADITIONAL COLONIAL.

[ABOVE] A ROUND TABLE MEANS NO SHARP CORNERS TO BUMP INTO IN THIS CITY KITCHEN. THE EATING AREA DOES DOUBLE DUTY AS PASSAGEWAY TO THE BACKYARD.

[OPPOSITE] UNCOMMON SEATING: AN OVERSIZED TABLE AND BENCH AND TWO VINTAGE PENDANTS ADD UNIQUE AMBIENCE IN THIS KITCHEN.

A variation on the standard table is the banquette, from the French word for "bench." This setup squeezes a lot of seating into a tight space—tucked into a corner or nestled beneath a bay window. Instead of chairs with arms and backs, a banquette uses built-in booth seating, as in a diner, which cuts down on floor and air space. Banquettes are usually custom-made to your specifications, so they'll fit to the inch.

Just because banquettes take up less room than traditional tables, however, doesn't mean they can't serve a crowd if they're big enough. Unlike a table, a banquette's fixed seat calls for just enough room to slide in and out (make sure the seat's fabric has enough slip!). Besides, people tend to squish close together in a booth. One family with young children built a 42-inch corner banquette into their busy kitchen to accommodate six comfortably, eight in a squeeze. The kids think the booth is the best seat in the house!

TRADE TIP

A banquette's built-in bench offers the opportunity to tuck in a little extra storage underneath, in a cabinet whose door is fashioned either to flip up like a trunk or pull out like a captain's bed.

[ABOVE] A BANQUETTE CAN ACCOMMODATE MORE BODIES (ESPECIALLY SMALL ONES) THAN CHAIRS CAN IN THE SAME SPACE. TO MAKE SLIDING IN EASY, CHOOSE A FABRIC THAT DOESN'T GRAB OR TWIST.

[RIGHT] A TABLE NEEDN'T SIT FREE-FLOATING IN THE CENTER OF A ROOM, WHERE IT CAN CREATE A RESTAURANT-LIKE ATMOSPHERE. PLACED AGAINST A WALL (AND IDEALLY UNDER A WINDOW), A TABLE FEELS MORE GROUNDED AND COZY.

The Appliances

Appliances are the guts and the glamour of a kitchen. In their most modern iterations, they're models of speed, efficiency, and power—some might argue, even of grace and beauty. Given freezers capable of supplying a banquet hall, restaurant-style refrigerators with glass doors, and drawers that warm food or chill wine, it's safe to say that appliances have evolved so much, both technologically and aesthetically, that they require some serious sizing up.

Appliances are, in fact, a wise starting point for any kitchen plan. Trust me: If you do the appliance research first, you'll avoid costly redos during the design or construction process. By virtue of their dimensions, appliances set the parameters for the rest of the kitchen design, from the number of cabinets to the length of the countertops. Stoves, refrigerators, and dishwashers come in a handful of standard sizes that can't be manipulated. A kitchen layout has to work around them, not vice versa. You can't shave a few inches off a range, for example, the way you can off a wood cabinet. If you leave appliance shopping to the end, you may find yourself short on room for that six-burner stove or the two separate cooling units—refrigerator and freezer—you have your heart set on.

Choosing appliances is undoubtedly a big decision. These big-ticket items eat up a major part of the kitchen's budget. They live large in the kitchen, taking up a fair amount of floor space. And they come in a wide range of style and color choices. When you walk into a showroom, the options can be overwhelming—and not just for the big three: the range, refrigerator, and dishwasher. Your options may also include beverage centers, warming drawers, microwaves, compactors, and complex venting systems.

To narrow the field, consider your agenda. Do you want a refrigerator roomy enough to accommodate a turkey platter? Sometimes I think entire kitchens are designed around that once-a-year 25-pound bird! Would you prefer a professional-style range or an understated, sleek, slide-in model? And when it comes to a dishwasher, is silence worth paying more for? Maybe you've always fantasized about your own flower sink or a second demi-dishwasher. A well-thought-out appliance plan can make the pipe dream real.

No matter what, think about what *you* need or desire, not what's new or trendy. A few years ago, all my clients requested a pasta-pot spigot near the stove, but most of the spigots ended up as props, not practical, day-to-day amenities. If the device du jour doesn't mesh with your cooking style, it is an unnecessary expense.

[OPPOSITE] AN OVERSIZE RANGE CALLS FOR AN OVERSIZE SPACE TO FIT IT INTO. WITH A 48-INCH RANGE, OR ANY RANGE FOR THAT MATTER, YOU NEED TO ADD AT LEAST 6 MORE INCHES TO BE MOST EFFECTIVE. THAT ALLOWS FOR A 3-INCH OVERHANG ON EACH SIDE.

Refrigerators: The Big Box

The refrigerator has often been the behemoth in the kitchen, but it need not be. It can be elegant and slender. It can be chic. It can even disappear, if it's a so-called built-in clad in cabinet doors that match the surrounding woodwork.

The first refrigeration decision is how it will fit into your plan. Refrigerators range from as narrow as 24 inches (refrigeration only) to as broad as 48 inches (side-by-side refrigerator-freezer). When choosing the size and style of your fridge, you have to factor in the size and style of your family. Are you stocking food for a brood of five, or just for you and a partner (human or canine)? Do you tend to stash a lot of meals in the freezer or do you shop daily and need plenty of space for fresh food in the crisper?

All of these decisions will influence your basic choice between freestanding or built-in. Freestanding models—the kind most of us grew up with—are easy to install (just plug in) and have the advantage of being readily available at modest price points. But from a visual standpoint, they stick out; literally, they project beyond the front face of your cabinets by up to 7 inches. The compressor, the housing for the coils, is built into the back of these units, so they can't sit flush against the wall. For this reason, most renovators and homeowners building a new kitchen don't like to install freestanding models. If you're replacing an existing machine and are locked into that exact size, however, the freestanding fridge is still a viable option.

Built-in refrigerators, my preference from a visual and practical viewpoint, sit perfectly even with the countertop, creating a unified, seamless kitchen perimeter. (Their close cousins, known as cabinet-depth units, project only as far as the dimension of the door.) Built-ins sit flush because their compressors are located on top, or occasionally at the bottom, of the unit instead of

TRADE TIP

Cabinet-clad refrigerators look handsome but can be hefty since the weight of the wood is added to the already substantial door—an issue for the very young or old. Be sure to choose a handle that's strong and big enough to get a firm grip on, which helps in tugging the door open.

at the back. This adds significant height. Built-ins, in fact, are typically 84 inches high, a full foot taller than most freestanding models (and the reason you can't simply swap one for the other). Most people find their kitchens can easily accommodate the taller units—if that inaccessible cabinet over the fridge has to be sacrificed, so be it; it's not exactly your most usable cabinet. Not surprisingly, built-ins are expensive—double or even triple the cost of basic, bulkier freestanding models.

Still, if the budget allows, flush refrigerators are worth it. They're the acknowledged standard of good design, sleek-looking and user friendly. The shallower shelves mean no scary leftovers lurking in the deep, dark cave at the back of the fridge. Built-ins have become so technologically advanced that some models come with dual refrigeration systems. These super-efficient units have two compressors, one for the fridge and one for the freezer, which means double insurance against breakdown (if one compressor goes on the fritz, you've got a backup going). They also save on energy, since each compressor runs only when needed. In addition, because the fridge and the freezer each have their own cooling unit, there's no chance of air or odor transferring from the fresh-food compartment to the freezer, as frequently happens when the compressor is shared. The practical upshot: no onion-infused ice cubes!

The size of a refrigerator, of course, influences the configuration—namely, where the freezer sits. If you are squeezed for space and can accommodate nothing larger than a 30- or 36-inch refrigerator, it's probably best to look at a model with a freezer on the bottom or top; at a narrow width, a side-by-side would give you only a sliver of refrigeration—forget about the turkey platter! While built-ins are always designed with bottom freezers, the freestanding models are available in both configurations. Personally, I prefer the freezer below, where it's out

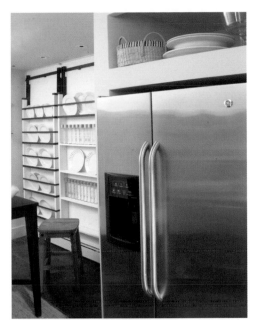

[LEFT] NEITHER FULLY BUILT IN NOR COMPLETELY FREESTANDING, THIS HYBRID FRIDGE (REFERRED TO AS "CABINET-DEPTH") WAS GIVEN ITS OWN WALL SPACE SO IT WOULDN'T STICK OUT. THE EXTRA SPACE BETWEEN THE TOP OF THE FRIDGE AND THE CEILING WAS PUT TO GOOD USE, AS A SHELVING NICHE FOR OVER-SIZED PLATTERS AND TRAYS.

[BELOW] IF YOU'RE BRAVE ENOUGH TO PUT YOUR EATING HABITS ON DIS-PLAY AND DISCIPLINED ENOUGH TO THROW OUT THE WILTED VEGGIES, THEN A GLASS-DOORED FRIDGE CAN ADD JUST THE RIGHT LIGHTNESS AND BRIGHTNESS TO YOUR KITCHEN.

TRADE TIP

When you order your refrigerator, don't forget to supply this key detail: the way you want the door to swing—left or right. For right-handed people, a handle on the left is more comfortable, but you also have to think about how the swing of the door affects the unloading of items and the flow of traffic. You don't want the door opening into a corridor between you and the sink or, on the other hand, banging into a countertop.

of the way. When you open the door to this style of fridge, you can quickly scan all the food at eye level, and the little ones in the house can independently reach the frozen treats.

Another type of fridge opens armoire-style, with double doors on top and a single freezer drawer below. This model is especially smart if you've got narrow clearance in your kitchen and don't want the door to swing too far out into the room. A pair of doors opens only 18 inches (half of a single swing of 36 inches), which logistically gives your kitchen more circulation space and may even allow you to add a few prized inches to an island or table.

Once you go wider than 36 inches, you move firmly into side-by-side territory. If you're on the fence about ordering the 42-inch or the 48-inch model, my advice is to always go bigger. For a modest increase in price, a few extra inches can make a significant difference in storing items, especially on the freezer side. If you have lots of room and need plenty of freezer space, you can even mix and match: Install two autonomous units (called *independent* or *freedom* units by the pros) next to each other, one all freezer, the other all refrigeration. Independents come in a surprising range of widths—18 to 36 inches—allowing you to customize your storage needs. But remember, you'll be doubling those dimensions to get separate fridge and freezer space. You need a very large kitchen to handle independents plus all the usual appliances, cabinets, and seating.

The final decision about the refrigerator is probably the first thing you notice: the finish. Standard laminates and pricier retro-chic porcelains give you the option of color—and it's not simply a matter of black or white. Stainless steel looks sleek but shows fingerprints, a consideration for the cleaning-obsessed (among whom I count myself). Speaking of neatness, glass-fronted styles, inspired by restaurant models, make a real statement, though they require a certain amount of artful arranging to keep the contents, perpetually in view, in order. Of course, you could just turn off the interior lights, and no one would be the wiser.

Then there's the custom approach: Built-in refrigerators allow you to slide a panel over the existing front, sheathing the door and drawer in any number of finishes. All manufacturers offer stock choices (stainless steel, black or white matte laminate), whereas some of the higher-priced manufacturers offer colors ranging from crisp red to bottle green and even oil-rubbed bronze. If you want a low-profile refrigerator, there's also the option of installing matching panels supplied by your cabinetmaker so your refrigerator blends in with the surrounding cabinetry. You can even cover the fridge's metal grille with cabinetry. To complete the camouflage, you can replace the standard door pull with hardware that matches the rest of the kitchen's cabinets. One client's son is amused because his friends can never find the fridge!

[TOP] A FAMILY FRIENDLY SETUP: THIS REFRIGERATOR, FLANKED BY PANTRY SPACE ON EITHER SIDE, HAS A FREEZER ON THE BOTTOM, SO KIDS CAN HELP THEMSELVES TO SNACKS AND DRINKS.

[ABOVE] ILLOGICAL AS IT SOUNDS, A FRIDGE MAY BE BETTER POSITIONED AT ONE END OF THE KITCHEN, NEAR THE FAMILY ROOM AND AWAY FROM THE CENTER OF THE ACTION AND COOKING—ESPECIALLY IN A FAMILY WITH LOTS OF KIDS WHO LIKE TO GET UNDERFOOT.

FIELD NOTE

You'd think, given the opportunity to renovate not one, not two, but three kitchens in the span of six years, the peripatetic Foley family would opt for the latest and greatest appliances in an effort to top themselves. Instead, time and time (and time) again, they chose the same straightforward model: a 36-inch gas range with a single oven, four burners, and a stainless-steel griddle. During the second and then the third renovation, they flirted with adding a second oven or a self-cleaning feature or swapping the griddle for a grill. But with their experience of turning out countless holiday meals for an extended family of twenty-five, they decided not to trade up when their relatively modest model served their needs. To keep from feeling utterly redundant, they ordered the stove in a succession of colors: blue (New York), then black (Maine), then white (Atlanta).

MAKING THE MICROWAVE FIT IN

The microwave has been around for quite some time, yet it's still hard to find the right place for it in kitchen plans. Most people plunk a microwave on the counter, near an outlet, where it takes up precious space and adds little to the countertop aesthetic. Some choose to install an over-the-range microwave that incorporates the exhaust hood—a look that works best if both the range and the kitchen are small. Over-the-range microwaves generally are no wider than 30 inches, not big or powerful enough to hold their own when installed over a pro-style range.

A built-in microwave (which comes with a clunky trim kit) can nestle into an open-fronted cabinet shelf, but that's not a perfect answer either, as it can make the upper cabinets look less streamlined and gobble up valuable eye-level accessible storage space. One workable solution: Order extra-deep upper cabinets to make room for a microwave behind closed doors. You'll be able to use the second shelf to store over-sized dishes above it as well. (Just keep in mind that your base cabinets may also need to be made deeper so you don't bang your head as you lean in to work.) Better yet, ask your contractor to recess the microwave into the wall studs by cutting out the interior back of the cabinet behind the microwave.

Cooktops and Ranges

The stove is often the central ingredient in a kitchen. You could say it's the hearth of the room—all the more so if it incorporates a chimney surround. Yet warmth is not all that counts. Whether you're a passionate or a part-time cook, the stove has to work well, and on many levels.

First, you should decide whether you want an all-in-one range—a freestanding unit that sits on the ground, with burners on top and an oven below—or whether you want to divide and conquer, installing a separate cooktop on the counter or island and an individual oven (or two) set into a wall or slipped under a counter.

The size of the range depends a great deal on the layout of the kitchen—and vice versa. Ranges run from 30 to 60 inches wide at price points from reasonable to stratospheric. Because the stove will most likely intersect a countertop, the bigger it is, the more countertop (not to mention cabinet space) it will eat up. Once you move into 36-inch ranges and larger, you're generally in the pro realm. While there's no technical definition for what constitutes a professional or restaurant-style range, most come with an extra oven (great for dinner party prep) and additional burners—up to eight, twice the standard four. These burners also get hotter than standard ones—15,000 BTUs (a measure of heat) versus the usual 4,000 or 5,000 BTUs—which means you can sear a steak or piece of fish more quickly and professionally. Frankly, I think anything over six burners is best reserved for restaurants. How much cooking do most of us usually do? If you have the luxury of room, six burners makes a lot of sense, as you can allocate the center burners for modular accessories—a built-in griddle or rotisserie, a grill, a deep fryer, or a wok, all amenities worth considering. At my house, we use our griddle for weekend pancakes and our grill for winter-weather grilling. They are both indispensable to our at-home cooking.

When it comes to the fuel itself, you have a choice of gas or electricity. Electric burners are hard to control with any subtlety.

[ABOVE] FINDING ROOM FOR A SECOND OVEN IN A KITCHEN WITH A PAUCITY OF WALL AND COUNTER SPACE IS TRICKY BUT NOT IMPOSSIBLE. THIS MODEL SLIDES RIGHT UNDER THE COUNTER, TAKING THE PLACE OF A BASE CABINET WHILE LEAVING THE COUNTERTOP UNENCUMBERED.

This can spell critical lag time for a serious cook. Electromagnetic or induction cooking (which has been around for decades in Europe but is still relatively novel in the United States) works by means of electricity-powered high-frequency magnetic coils that "induce" heat, heating the pot while the burners themselves stay magically cool to the touch. This type of cooktop is gaining ground among chefs who value induction's ability to heat in a nanosecond and clean in a snap. What's more, the units are made of glass ceramic and have an exceptionally sleek and minimalist profile.

Still, my preference, hands down, is for the gas burner, which responds immediately to small changes in flame. I'm the doubting Thomas type who needs to see the flame to know the stove is working. Gas burners are available with a choice of grates, including star-shaped (to distribute heat evenly) and claw-shaped (so the pot sits higher over the flame, as with a bona fide restaurant unit). I'm partial to cooktops with one smooth continuous grate, which allows you to slide pots effortlessly across the surface. When ordering, you'll also need to specify whether you want the gas burners to be open or sealed. The sealed ones are easier to clean—no bubbled-over soup or stew dribbling into the stove's inner workings. Some cooks prefer open burners on the theory that the additional air around the flame allows for more heat. Because most ranges have an excess of BTUs, however, I'd opt for sealed. In either case, you should look for a burner with a fully adjustable flame, one that can lick the sides of a pan impressively and then quiet down to a low glow for simmering.

Electric ovens, on the other hand, have a slight advantage over gas. Once the temperature is set, electric ovens vary by only 4 to 6 degrees, while gas models can fluctuate up to 25 degrees. Due to this even heat, electric ovens are better for roasting and baking than gas ovens. Many range manufacturers feature models with a best-of-both-worlds feature called *dual fuel*—gas burners on top of an electric oven—though these are pricier than standard gas-oven/gas-burner models. No matter your fuel choice, order the widest oven your layout will allow. Stand-alone 30-inch wall ovens accommodate large cookie sheets and roasting pans with ease, but the 24- and 27-inch models do not. For a lot of cooking versatility in one neat bundle, I like what my own kitchen designer calls the triple stack—either oven-plus-oven-plus-warming drawer or oven-plus-warming drawer-plus-microwave/convection oven placed one on top of the other. It sounds like a tall order, but the stack fits comfortably in a kitchen with an 8-foot ceiling. There's even room for a cabinet above and a slim drawer below. The bottom drawer has the added advantage of raising the lowest member of the stack off the floor.

Convection, of course, is another cooking category. This type of oven—both all-convection-all-the-time models and regular ovens with a convection button you can flip on as needed—has the advantage of speed. A fan circulates hot air throughout the interior (rather than having the fan cycle on and off, as with most ovens), so food cooks at a completely even temperature. Convections come in two flavors, as it were, American and European. The American style uses two powerful fans, which

[TOP] YOU CAN SPRAY YOUR RANGE ANY COLOR YOU LIKE, PROVIDED YOU HAVE IT DONE PROFESSIONALLY, USING THE SAME HEAT-RESISTANT PAINTS THEY USE TO SPRAY CARS! THIS CUSTOM CLARET RANGE PROVED SO PLEASING THAT VIKING INCORPORATED IT INTO THEIR COLOR LINE.

[ABOVE] A DROP-IN STOVETOP IS SET SMARTLY BACK FROM THE ISLAND EDGE AND BORDERED IN AN EXOTIC ZEBRA WOOD.

cooks food 30 percent faster than conventional ovens. Available only in electric convection ovens, the European style has a single heating fan that sucks the air backward and burns it clean before recirculating it. This means odors don't transfer from rack to rack. You can simultaneously roast lamb and bake a berry cobbler without worrying about their flavors mixing or mingling.

Fast as they are, convection ovens take some getting used to. You have to adjust recipes, reducing both oven temperature (by about 20 percent) and cooking time (by about 25 percent). Some cooks grumble that the super-efficient fan dries food out, and that's true, if you forget to turn the heat down a bit. I learned the hard way: I had trouble trusting that the temperature should be turned down for cooking chicken. (Not so my husband, who got the convection concept immediately and always cooks the chicken just right.) However, who can complain about less cooking time and therefore less fuel—a feel-good "green" bonus?

For small meals and small spaces, you can augment your big (or non) convection oven with a convection-style microwave. These units combine the swiftness of a microwave with convection's ability to brown food. They're ideal for quick summer meals (roast chicken, anyone?) when you don't want a whole oven heating up your kitchen.

Steam convection ovens are another quick cooking option, especially for the health-conscious (but not the cost-conscious; these ovens, which are mostly European, are pricy). Nothing compares to steam in terms of sealing in natural flavor, color, and vitamins and minerals. For example, fish steamed at a low temperature in this kind of convection oven stays tender yet develops a nice, crisp crust.

Just Venting

Hoods top off the stove in more than one way. They have a strong visual impact and a critical function: to ventilate.

While it sounds obvious, the most important consideration is matching the ventilation system to the heat output of the range or cooktop. Some renovators don't like the look of a heavy hood and are tempted to choose an unobtrusive model for the sake of design. Big mistake. The smell of grilled salmon or sautéed onions can linger for hours if not properly vented.

How much ventilation you need is a simple matter of math. Oven hoods are rated based on how much air they can move in a given amount of time. The standard measure is cubic feet of air per minute (CFM). The best professional hoods run up to 1,500 CFMs, while a generic type might run a mere 180 CFMs, barely enough to clear the steam from boiling pasta. My rule of thumb (and the advice of most appliance experts): A 30-inch range needs at least 600 CFMs; a 48-inch cooktop, 1,000 CFMs; and a grande dame 60-inch range, 1,500 CFMs.

The standard hood extends over the stove like a roof and functions like an umbrella, trapping smoke, grease, and odor. Placement is everything. The closer your vent system is to an exterior wall

[ABOVE] THIS GENEROUSLY SIZED HOOD, DETAILED WITH HANDSOME CEILING TRIM, WAS INSTALLED HIGH ABOVE THE COOKTOP TO ALLOW HANGING ROOM FOR BIGGER POTS AND LONGER PANS.

[OPPOSITE] A REAL PROFESSIONAL RANGE ALMOST NEEDS TO STAND ALONE AS THIS ONE DOES. THIRTY INCHES WERE PIRATED FROM THE ADJOINING LAUNDRY ROOM TO CREATE AN ACCOMMODATING RECESS.

WRAPAROUND WINDOWS WERE A GIVEN, BUT WHERE TO HANG THE OVEN HOOD? IN A BOLD MOVE, THE MULLANEYS CENTERED A FREE-HANGING OVEN HOOD IN FRONT OF A WINDOW.

and the fewer turns the ductwork makes en route to the outside, the more effectively the hood will work. When ordering, make sure the hood reaches at least 1 inch beyond the burners on each side for maximum drawing power.

If your cooktop is going to be placed in a center island, you have to address the topic of downdraft ventilation. Downdrafts sound great in theory. A fan unit recessed within a base cabinet rises behind the cooktop with the push of a button, ready to ensnare smoke and steam at their source. While pots bubbling away on the back burners do benefit (if only slightly) from the fan, the front burners hardly benefit at all. The reason is, of course, that smoke rises—so as clever as downdrafts are, they simply cannot match the odor-catching quality of a good hood. Downdrafts catch a mere 20 percent of fumes and grease, while over-the-oven hoods catch up to 75 percent.

A more efficient ventilation solution is to suspend a hood from the ceiling directly over the island's cooktop. The floating hood, designed to be viewed from all sides (unlike those anchored to the wall behind a range), can look either clumsy and intrusive or, in the right space (a large one), dramatic. If you're hanging a hood over an island and you don't want it to look heavy or to block your sight lines, hang it above eye level.

The look of any hood depends largely on what it's encased in, from the most common material, stainless steel, to more unusual choices, such as copper, brass, and even powder-coated enamel. If you prefer an understated, integrated look, you can order what's called a wood hood blower. This type of mechanism is only the guts of the hood, not its outer shell, and it can be tucked right into a cabinet or hearth hung over a cooktop or range. The net result is you see the woodwork, not the hood.

Cleaning Up

Dishwashers

A dishwasher is invaluable, but it's not always the easiest appliance to live with, given its tendency to swish and clank away while you're trying to have a conversation or watch television. The best dishwashers are conspicuously, gloriously silent. These days, they're also environmentally conscious, using half the water and soap of the older models. The trade-off is a much longer running time, an inconvenience mitigated by the muffled noise.

But while silence is quite a perk—especially if the kitchen is open to the family room—I'd argue that the interior layout and capacity of the dishwasher are even more important. My favorite models have one thing in common: a smart and flexible loading design. One especially clever feature is a variable rack that you can raise (to make room for oversized plates on the bottom) or lower (to accommodate tall wine glasses on the top). A cutlery tray ordered from the dishwasher manufacturer is another small detail with considerable impact. The tray, which sits above the top shelf over the glassware, replaces the traditional silverware basket below, creating room to stack an additional six or so plates. Some units have such a capacious interior you can wash sixteen (rather than the standard twelve) place settings at once, without using more water. What's to lose?

As for getting dishes their absolute cleanest, look for models with extra programs and features that measure the level of dirtiness. If you're not sure what setting to use, you can let the dishwasher decide. Dishwashers now have enough wash action that you don't even need to rinse. (In fact, don't

[TOP] IN THIS DOUBLE-HEIGHT KITCHEN, THE OWNERS WOULD HAVE HAD TO INSTALL A HANGING OVEN HOOD THAT DESCENDED AN UN-WIELDY 6 FEET. INSTEAD, THEY INSTALLED A DOWNDRAFT VENT IN THE ISLAND THAT IT POPS UP AT THE TOUCH OF A BUTTON.

[ABOVE] A MINI-DISHWASHER HIDES BENEATH WHAT APPEARS TO BE AN ORDINARY DISH DRAIN.

rinse, or your dishwasher can start to etch the surface of your plates; it needs something to clean.) Some models offer the option of doing just half a load on the lower or upper rack only. How did dishwashers get so smart?

Dishwashers are so practical, you might want two! People who entertain a lot, or cook for a big family 24/7, often add a second dishwasher. As long as you're doubling up, it makes sense to look for an auxiliary model with special talents—a version made especially for pots and pans, in which the interior is less divided and the water runs hotter, for example, or a model designed to handle the full spectrum of stemware and fine china with TLC.

If you subscribe to the more-is-better theory but don't have room to install two full-fledged dishwashers, you might want to look into the dishwasher drawer option. Dishwasher drawers allow you to run small loads or to set one machine for rinsing glassware and the other for scrubbing bowls or pots. A boon in kosher kitchens, where meat and dairy dishes must be kept separate, the drawers are also finding an audience among those who generate few dishes, whether singletons or empty nesters.

Sinks

Choosing a sink may not be terribly exciting, but the sink happens to be the most used kitchen feature, bar none. We probably spend 75 percent of kitchen time at or near the sink (or more, it seemed, when my children were little), so naturally you want to choose a sink you'll like standing at. I've had both single and double sinks, and each has its pluses and minuses. A single large sink provides a generous basin in which to soak large pots and pans—great for a large family or one that entertains a lot. However, when the pans are steeping, the whole sink is out of commission. A double sink allows you to soak a few things on one side while scraping and rinsing on the other—great if you're willing to clean as you go. However, neither side is really big enough for large baking sheets or roasting pans.

Whether you choose a single or double sink, you still have to settle on the size. To me, the ideal sink dimensions are 21 inches from left to right and 18 inches from front to back, give or take a few inches either way. Many people I know love going even wider—up to 30 inches wide, so the basin can accommodate an entire dinner party's worth of dishes. (The front-to-back measurement is less variable, since you are limited by your cabinet's depth.) As for the depth of the sink itself, I find the standard 6 or 8 inches too shallow, though bending over a deep sink can be a pain in the back. A sink about 10 inches deep is a happy medium.

TRADE TIP

If you plan to use a wood panel to disguise the dishwasher door as cabinetry, ask about ordering a heavy-duty hinge (standard in European models; an option on American models). Wood panels add considerable weight and have a tendency to tug the dishwasher door out of alignment after repeated openings.

[ABOVE] A FULLY INTEGRATED DISHWASHER COMES WITH A HIDDEN CONTROL PANEL AND CAN BE TOTALLY CAMOUFLAGED WITH A CABINETRY PANEL. EVEN THE HANDLE CAN BE MATCHED TO THE REST OF THE KITCHEN'S HARDWARE.

FIELD NOTE

Sometimes an entire kitchen renovation can start with the kitchen sink. The Chang-Scanlan family in Greenwich, Connecticut, initially planned to hook up the main sink in a typical spot—under a pair of windows facing the backyard. Pretty as the view would be, Cynthia Chang didn't like the idea of having her back to the kitchen and her family every time she did the dishes. Why not put the sink in the island, the designer suggested, in the center of the action? That would work, she reasoned, but what of the family's passion for organic gardening? Cynthia didn't relish the idea of dirt-covered heads of lettuce and stalks of beans overtaking her new sink in the island. After scrutinizing the plan—again—she and her architect found a convenient spot for a large second sink right by the back door.

As for the shape of the sink, a rectangle is most familiar, but other geometrics hold their own. You can find circles and D-shapes (half-circles on the back side, straight and squared off in the front). You can find square sinks, too. It's hip to be square; a popular model features a compartment with a suspended drain for easy rinsing and dish-drainer drying. In an innovative move, one family had two identical squares undermounted side by side in their stone countertop. A small strip of the stone was routed out to create a trough between the sinks in case of overflow—a clever and original design.

Speaking of doubling up, you might also consider a second sink in a separate location—the classic prep sink. A common misconception is that prep sinks are by definition small. I like them big—at least 13 inches round or 15 inches square; any smaller and they look like a toy and function as such. Prep sinks come in more shapes and finishes than you might expect, from simple stainless-steel circles to, at the other extreme, a scullery-like rectangular basin with a hammered or aged finish. Whichever type you choose, be sure it sits back far enough on your countertop (at least 4 inches, as compared to the standard 1 or 2), as its diminutive stature means the faucet will be close at hand—too much so.

The material a sink is fabricated from is another key consideration, and your decision may well come down to durability, design, price, or some combination of all three. Among the top choices:

- Stainless steel. Stainless is prized for its strength. You can measure quality by thickness, also known as gauge; ironically, the lower the number, the higher the quality—that is, the thicker it will be. The strongest and most dentproof stainless sinks are in the 12-gauge range. Stainless sinks that incorporate other metals, such as steel chromium and nickel, are especially durable and seen as the top of the line. To avoid the inevitable scratches, look for a brushed finish. Always classic looking, stainless is not strictly a modern choice; it is actually historically appropriate for older homes and was frequently the sink of choice in homes built in the 1920s, '30s, and '40s.

- Porcelain. Pearly porcelain over cast iron can have either a vintage appeal (think farmhouse chic) or a sleek, modern sensibility. Porcelain is one of the most popular materials for sinks, given its wide range of colors. Be careful when cleaning porcelain, however, particularly in white, as it's prone to chip when subjected to heavy-duty cleansers. In a slightly different vein, consider enameled cast iron (versus plain old enamel) as another handsome and durable choice. Beware, however, that these sinks are heavy and may need an underlying structure to support them, which takes a bite out of the under-cabinet storage space.

- **Enamel.** The big advantage—and it's significant—is cost. Enamel sinks are less expensive than almost any other variety but also less durable. Think about enamel for a second sink that doesn't get daily use, as it's prone to chipping.

- **Solid surfacing.** You can integrate sinks that are fashioned from solid surfacing resins—Corian and its cousins—right into the countertop so there is no definition between where one ends and the other begins. While practical, they have a habit of looking rather odd—like an iris-less eye.

- **Stone.** Marble, granite, or soapstone sinks make a big impact in a kitchen, particularly when they are fashioned into extra-deep farm-style sinks. Stone, of course, is expensive, but you can also specify any size, shape, and depth. Be mindful that the same maintenance issues come into play with a stone sink as with a stone counter: Marble is more prone to staining than granite, and soapstone requires frequent oiling to keep its mellow patina. Quartz composites, the new stone sink on the block, are the sturdiest of the lot.

- **Copper or brass.** These warm metallics usually appear in small prep sinks on an island or bar, but you can think out of the box—and the kitchen. An oversized copper farmhouse sink can make for a practical and dramatic feature in a mudroom or a potting shed.

Faucets

A sink doesn't serve much of a purpose without a faucet! As utilitarian as faucets are, however, they're surprisingly versatile in style: vintage spigots, commercial sprayers, gooseneck models, pull-out wands that adjust from spray to rain and back again. Some purists like the look of separate hot and cold faucets, but the more practical choice is a single lever with integrated hot and cold water, which allows you to temper the temperature—to cold, cool, lukewarm, or hot. A swiveling spigot is almost de rigueur, and if you have a double basin, be sure your faucet pivots a full 180 degrees to service both sinks (lesson learned from experience: My faucet swings more easily to the smaller side sink than the main sink, where the lever interferes). An independent sprayer or a pull-out faucet is indispensable, in my opinion.

[TOP] SIDE-BY-SIDE STYLE: A PAIR OF GENEROUSLY SIZED BASINS OFFERS A CHIC ALTERNATIVE TO THE STANDARD DOUBLE SINK, IN WHICH ONE SIDE IS BIGGER THAN THE OTHER. ONE SIDE IS USED FOR WASHING; THE OTHER IS OUTFITTED WITH A RACK FOR DRIP-DRYING.

[CENTER] A SHALLOW SINK IN A BEAUTIFUL SILVER FINISH IS MEANT FOR LIGHT USE, WHETHER RINSING A FLUTED GOBLET OR LETTING A FEW ICE CUBES MELT.

[BOTTOM] IN A KITCHEN WITH CARRERA MARBLE COUNTERS, A SINK CUSTOM-CARVED FROM THE SAME SLAB CREATES A UNIFIED AND UNUSUAL LOOK. CUSTOM ALSO MEANS THAT YOU CAN MAKE THE BASIN AS DEEP AND WIDE AS YOU WANT. THIS CUSTOM-CARVED CARRERA MARBLE SINK IS BIG ENOUGH FOR THE OWNER'S COLLECTION OF RUSSIAN COPPER POTS. KEEP IN MIND THAT BECAUSE A SINK IS USUALLY WET, THE STONE WILL READ DARKER THAN THE SURROUNDING COUNTER.

TRADE TIP

How do you want your sink to relate to your countertop? The most common answer is to mount a self-rimming or drop-in sink with a lip that overhangs the countertop slightly. The rim has the advantage of protecting the counter from moisture damage—a logical choice for laminates and woods. But it also has a significant disadvantage: Crumbs and morsels collect around the rim. Undermount sinks, by contrast, are installed from below—and without a lip, there's no place for grime to collect. Because the edges of the countertop show with this type of installation, undermounts are limited to either stone or solid-surface countertops (inherently more expensive options than other countertop materials). Cleanup is a breeze, since you can sweep food right into the sink.

Farmhouse or apron-front sinks are a third option. These sinks are finished with an exposed apron in front, while the counter generally extends a bit over the sink on the sides. Farmhouse sinks were once available only in porcelain but are now made in stainless steel, stone, and other materials.

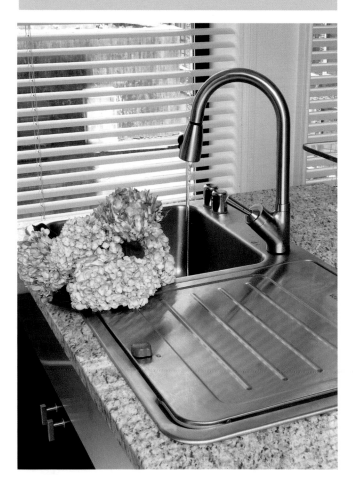

TRADE TIP

Look for dishwashers (refrigerators, too, for that matter) with the official Energy Star label, which signifies reduced water and electricity consumption.

[ABOVE] LAMINATES REPLACED THE WOOD AND STAINLESS-STEEL COUNTERS OF EARLY-TWENTIETH-CENTURY KITCHENS. SOONER OR LATER LAMINATES CHIP, CRACK, AND DELAMINATE; THEY ARE INEXPENSIVE AND EASY TO REPLACE, BUT IMPOSSIBLE TO REPAIR.

[LEFT] IN A CITY APARTMENT, A STAINLESS-STEEL LIP ENCAPSULATES A DROP-IN SINK AND (SURPRISE!) A COMPANION IN-COUNTER TOPLOADING DISHWASHER.

Another determining faucet factor: How many holes do you want sunk into your countertop? If you have chosen a drop-in sink model, the matter is likely decided for you. These sinks have predrilled holes—from one hole (for a single lever) to five holes (for a separate hot-and-cold model with room for a sprayer and another accessory). If you are having your sink undermounted into stone or solid-surface counters, you can select the number of holes. I vote for three: one for a single-lever faucet, another for a sprayer, and a third for a built-in soap dispenser, to keep plastic bottles off the countertop and to encourage family handwashing. Some of my clients are partial to the instant hot water dispensers, but I've never warmed to them. Not only are they energy inefficient, they're redundant. If the kitchen has a high-powered stove, you can already heat water nearly instantaneously.

As for spigot styles, they run the gamut from classic to über-modern. You may like the long, elegant look of a gooseneck—which has the distinctive advantage of being able to fill the tallest pots—or the simplicity of a more compact, modern design. The best-quality

TRADE TIP

The higher the faucet spout and the deeper the sink, the greater the pull of gravity— and the subsequent splatter. Another height consideration: Shallow basins need taller spigots so you can fit a pasta pot underneath the spout.

faucets are made of noncorrosive solid brass, but that isn't necessarily the finish you see. The sink manufacturers then plate that solid brass base finish with chrome, nickel, or whatever suits your style. While chrome is the industry standard, and perfectly fine by me, you can go up in price with elegant nickel or unlacquered brass finishes. For kitchens that lean toward the craftsman or cottage style, I'm partial to the weathered patina of oil-rubbed bronze.

The Extras

No one *needs* a pizza oven. No one *needs* a wine fridge, either (unless you're a vintner, of course), but it's the kind of amenity that can make an otherwise commonplace kitchen feel luxurious. The following auxiliary appliances have won raves from many of my clients, who have said they would order them all over again.

Beverage Centers These resourceful units slide under the countertop in widths from 15 to 24 inches. The best ones have completely adjustable racks, allowing you to store a combination of beverages, from cans of soda to a few bottles of bordeaux. By moving drinks out of the primary fridge, you free up valuable

[ABOVE] EVEN A SMALL KITCHEN CAN BE DESIGNED FOR ENTERTAINING. HERE, AN UNDER-COUNTER BEVERAGE CENTER AT THE END OF THE PENINSULA STORES WINE FOR PARTIES.

[LEFT] FOR AN ENTHUSIAST, A SMALL FRIDGE MAY NOT BE ENOUGH. THIS FAMILY PLANS TO INSTALL A TALLER UNIT, CONVERTING THE MINI-FRIDGE TO A BEVERAGE "BAR" FOR THE KIDS.

[OPPOSITE] YOU CAN SLIP DRAWERS FOR SPECIALIZED COOLING INTO A VARIETY OF UNDERCOUNTER SPOTS.

shelf space. Plus, kids can grab a cold drink without getting underfoot. They offer about the same overall refrigeration—5 or 6 cubic feet—as a pair of built-in refrigerator drawers for a fraction of the price.

Wine Storage

If you're a wine lover, a mini wine cellar right in your kitchen makes sense—more sense, certainly, than lining up bottles in the fridge, where they consume food space, or shoving them on a closet shelf, where they might get knocked over. For many of the benefits of a wine cellar minus the construction hassle, look into either full-height or undercounter wine cabinets. All are designed to store bottles horizontally, keeping the corks moist. The preeminent models have three distinct temperate zones (40 to 65 degrees) to store white, reds, and bubblies at their ideal temperatures. The smallest cabinets have room for 30 bottles, while the largest stock upward of 150. Because fluctuations in light or movement can ruin a good wine, higher-end units have special glass to keep out UV rays and a compressor to minimize vibrations. As a bonus, wine coolers also happen to store wine's classic accompaniment, cheese, at its proper humidity.

Warming Drawers

Many homeowners rationalize warming drawers by thinking they will prove handy for entertaining—and they do. But clients with busy lives and after-school-activity-crazed children find them useful on a daily basis. These drawers are invaluable for keeping weeknight dinners warm (but not dried out) for whoever is running late. In fact, in my neck of the woods, local lore has it that late one evening on a Metro-North train, a group of commuters were lamenting going home to dried-out microwaved dinners; a fellow passenger piped up and told them that in his house, late dinners were kept moist and hot in a warming drawer. Next thing you know, appliance stores were touting the Metro-North Warming Drawer. A warming drawer keeps food warm and moist for

[LEFT] GATHER AROUND THE WATERCOOLER . . . OR WINE COOLER. A GENEROUS ADJUNCT TO A KITCHEN ALLOWS ROOM FOR BOTH, WITH STORAGE AND COUNTERTOP AT HAND.

[ABOVE] A WARMING DRAWER CAN BE INCORPORATED INTO A STOVETOP, COUPLED WITH A WALL OVEN, OR INSTALLED AS A STAND-ALONE UNIT. WHEREVER IT FINDS A HOME, HOWEVER, I DON'T KNOW OF A SINGLE CUSTOMER WHO DOESN'T RESPOND WARMLY TO OWNING ONE.

[OPPOSITE] CONSIDER THE FINISH AND THE MAINTENANCE FACTOR WHEN CHOOSING AN APPLIANCE. STAINLESS STEEL REQUIRES A CONSCIENTIOUS EFFORT TO KEEP IT LOOKING LIKE NEW. GLASS DOORS PRESENT YET ANOTHER POTENTIAL DRAWBACK: EVERYTHING INSIDE IS ALWAYS ON VIEW.

three to five hours—a significant improvement over an oven, in which food dries out in a mere 20 minutes.

Warming drawers can serve other roles in the kitchen. They allow you to work on several components of a meal sequentially—you can make one dish and put it on hold in the warming drawer while you move on to the next course. The most versatile models have a dividing rack, allowing you to stack multiple plates and tuck in a baking dish or two; and adjustable heat, from a mere 90 degrees (perfect for proofing dough) to 210 degrees (the ideal temperature for keeping food warm but not warmed over). Be sure to install the warming tray close to your ovens or cooktop for easy transfer. Who wants to carry a hot dish across the kitchen?

Refrigerator and Freezer Drawers

You can install small independent freezers and fridges to augment your basic big box, particularly if you have a big family or a big thirst, or entertain big crowds. They're easy to slip in anywhere in the room. Stocked with drinks or outfitted with produce crisper drawers, cold drawers cut down on the amount of time you leave your refrigerator door hanging ajar. Freezer drawers are the solution for the cook who wants to buy frozen steaks or store soup stock. And you can store kids' ice cream in a freezer drawer, keeping the regular freezer free of sticky hands. What's more, the ice-making part of freezer drawers constantly makes new cubes, so your ice is always fresh and crystal clear.

When you select your appliances, remember that you are making a long-term commitment. You're better off picking a quality brand and a known model rather than a hot new machine with up-to-the-minute technology. Don't be the first on your block to try the latest dishwasher that uses negative ions instead of water to clean your dishes (after all, those negative ions might affect the free radicals in your clothing or cause headaches) or the refrigerator with a computer and TV built into the door (the ones I've encountered thus far have always been out of order). Any new, high-tech appliance should weather a couple of seasons in the marketplace to make sure all the kinks are worked out, and that there's enough consumer demand to ensure it will stay in the line for some time to come. My advice: Buy the best you can afford with the conveniences that work for you and your family, and in a color you can live with—season after season.

GREEN MACHINES

These appliances are the unglamorous extras. The attraction comes from their strong ecological appeal.

- **TRASH COMPACTORS.** Compactors come in varying cubic capacities and are all quite reasonably priced. Trash compactors not only cut down on your family's garbage output but also the space your waste takes up in landfills. According to the Environmental Protection Agency (EPA), the average family member generates 10 pounds of household waste per week. For a family of six, that's more than 3,000 pounds in a year—the weight of a small car! A compactor reduces that waste to one and a half bags of garbage for an entire week—not to mention making garbage duty far less onerous . . . and odorous.

- **GARBAGE DISPOSALS.** Disposals are environmentally correct in that they remove a major component, food waste, from the landfill mix. Unfortunately, some communities, Manhattan included, can't accommodate disposal washout in their water mains. If you are allowed to install a disposal, go for a large one so you can toss all kinds of peels and pits down the drain without worrying about jamming.

Going green can be as simple as using fluorescent undercounter lighting; incandescent bulbs consume four times the electricity of fluorescent lights. Newer dishwasher models use less than half the water of their predecessors. Convection ovens cook 33 percent faster than conventional ovens, thus consuming 33 percent less electricity. These seemingly simple changes not only help with fuel consumption and environmental issues but will also pay for themselves in short order.

GREEN-PAINTED CABINETS AND RECYCLING ARE TWO WAYS OF "GOING GREEN." IN THIS KITCHEN THE OWNERS CHOSE TO KEEP THE OLD WAINSCOTING RATHER THAN JUST CARTING IT TO THE CURB. THAT'S GREEN, TOO.

COLOR SENSE

When it comes to choosing the shade or shine of appliances, most people tend to think in black and white, or perhaps stainless steel. But look twice, and you'll see the options are far broader.

THE CLASSICS Black or white are timeless and have the advantage of being unobtrusive and unassuming. If you want to make a strong statement, however, consider the range of hues available in the marketplace, from the richest (red, cobalt blue, eggplant) to the subtlest (buttercream, mint, gray). If you choose a color, a *real* color, for your appliances, you had better be committed for the long term. When I see a picture of a siren-red kitchen in a magazine, I wonder what happens when the owners fall out of love with it. But if you know you're a blue person (and blue people usually really know it); then by all means opt for a blue refrigerator or range. Or if you are after a more nuanced look, check out appliances in restrained shades such as charcoal, putty, or taupe; they still say special, but in a subtler way. A stand-out stove in a small kitchen might be overpowering.

On the subject of standing out, you need to be selective. If you want strong-colored appliances, you might opt for a quieter, more understated surface for your countertops to keep the kitchen from looking too flamboyant.

STAINLESS STEEL The most requested finish choice for appliances, stainless adds a luxurious gleam to a kitchen that often belies the price; you can find a stainless-steel fridge for $400 or $4,000. In fact, stainless, once considered the ultimate status symbol, is now so accessible that over 25 percent of all kitchens have stainless appliances.

One of its main appeals is that stainless is always a consistent shade, so you're free to pick and choose your fridge, stove, and dishwasher from different manufacturers and still get a uniform look. On the downside, stainless shows every smudge and requires that you use a special spray cleaner and buff (not scrub) with a soft cloth, working in one direction. It's best to clean daily because a buildup of smudge has the habit of turning gummy and scummy. Titanium, touted as the new fingerprint-proof stainless steel, has never really caught on. Critics say it looks synthetic, and stainless die-hards say there's only one metal worth its mettle. Recently, a few manufacturers have introduced a true stainless-steel finish with an added topcoating. This new protected finish closely resembles the original and might be a good option for the finger-print phobic.

[OPPOSITE, ABOVE LEFT] FINALLY! NOW THERE ARE FINGERPRINT-PROOF AND MAR-RESISTANT STAINLESS-STEEL FINISHES—OR ARE THEY? LABELED "TITANIUM" OR "CLEAN STEEL" BY THEIR MANUFACTURERS, THESE SMUDGE-PROOF "STAINLESS" MODELS ARE REALLY JUST PLAIN GRAY PLASTIC.

[OPPOSITE, ABOVE RIGHT] SPECIAL CLEANERS ARE RECOMMENDED FOR SENSITIVE STAINLESS STEEL . BE SURE TO RUB IN ONE DIRECTION ONLY!

[OPPOSITE, BELOW LEFT] BRIGHT WHITE WOULD HAVE BEEN TOO HARSH AND CLINICAL FOR THIS COUNTRY FRENCH KITCHEN. VIKING'S WONDERFUL COLOR RANGE HAD JUST THE RIGHT "OLD" WHITE.

[OPPOSITE, BELOW RIGHT] A CLASSIC COMBINATION: THIS TRUE COMMERCIAL RANGE IN BLACK PUNCTUATES A WHITE KITCHEN. IF YOU'RE FEELING MORE DARING, EXPERIMENT WITH A COLORED RANGE. AND NOT TO WORRY—IF YOU TIRE OF A COLOR, YOU CAN HAVE YOUR APPLIANCE PROFESSIONALLY SPRAYED IN A DIFFERENT HUE (CHECK THE YELLOW PAGES).

The Cabinetry

The design of kitchen cabinetry is hardly an open and shut case. Cabinets, as a category—upper and undercounter storage units, doors and drawers, and, if you're lucky, an island or a peninsula—are multifaceted and multitasking. As the most conspicuous elements in the room, they not only help set the decorative tone of the space but also play a key utilitarian role as the workhorses of a kitchen— storing food and spices, holding dishes and flatware, hiding cookie sheets and stew pots from view.

Choosing cabinets that are good-looking and of good quality takes careful consideration. After all, they'll be hanging around a while; you don't tend to replace cabinetry as often as the machinery elements in a kitchen, like fridges and dishwashers (my cabinets are forty years old, my ovens merely two).

Before you make decisions about the cabinets—or even take measurements—take stock of the appliances you're buying and where they are going to be installed. It doesn't make sense to finalize the cabinet layout until you know the dimensions, placement, and cost of the refrigerator, stove, sink, and dishwasher. These hulking elements drive the mathematics of your cabinetry. Kitchen plans must be tightly orchestrated (see "The Layout," page 19, for details). Cabinets and drawers and doors must be calculated to the ⅛ inch or they won't fit, quite literally, around the appliances, windows, and walls.

Once you get your appliance specs in hand and establish the other parameters (including any limitations) of the space, you'll have a much clearer idea of how many

and what types of cabinets will fit. *Then* you can begin thinking about style. Do you want cabinets that are simple or embellished? with panels that are raised or recessed? painted or glazed or natural wood? with hidden or visible hinges? with handles or knobs? Do you imagine your kitchen ringed with upper cabinets, or would you prefer a more open, airy space, with lower cabinets only? In that case, you'll need to find storage space elsewhere in the kitchen. (Paging the pantry!)

It's not just the look of the cabinetry itself but how the cabinets are arranged that contribute to a kitchen's aesthetic. Designers and architects obsess over symmetry (I admit I am occasionally guilty, too). The old saw about making sure that all upper cabinets line up over their lower counterparts (so a 24- inch cabinet always sits over a 24-inch cabinet) is irrelevant, given all the warming drawers and wine coolers that interrupt a typical run of cabinetry. Still, even if cabinets don't end up perfectly paired, two by two, like in Noah's ark, the

[OPPOSITE] A RUBBED WAX FINISH LIKE THE ONE ON THESE PINE CABI-NETS IS BOTH WARM AND WONDER-FULLY FORGIVING. DINGS, SCRATCHES, AND GAUGES CAN BE MINIMIZED WITH AN AT-HOME WAXING (AL-THOUGH SOME HOMEOWNERS FEEL THEY SIMPLY ADD TO THE PATINA).

goal is to find a rhythm—a balance—so the overall effect is both pleasing and logical.

Shopping the Options

It's a known truth in the world of kitchen construction: Cabinetry accounts for a good solid half of the entire renovation ticket, so you can't tiptoe around the budget issue. When dealing with cabinetmakers, showrooms, or carpenters, it's wise to be as clear as you can from the outset about what you can allocate from your overall budget. The good news—and the sometimes tricky part—is that there are plenty of options in every price bracket. Kitchen cabinets come from all kinds of suppliers, from one-man carpentry shops to huge factories that turn out prefabricated units. My advice? Ask for advice. Comparing prices between types, not to mention between vendors or suppliers, is a complex business. Evaluations are rarely apples to apples. Still, you can usually boil cabinet expense down to a cost-per-linear-foot basis. A kitchen planner, a cabinetmaker, or the professionals in a showroom can help you navigate the choices as long as you're unequivocal about what you can spend.

The first decision you'll have to make is whether to go the ready-made or the custom-made route. Within these two broad categories lie some important differences. Ready-made cabinets are just that: They're predesigned, premade, and finished boxes, doors, and drawers that are sitting in stores, ready to be loaded on the car's roof rack. They come in standard industry increments—usually between 12 and 36 inches wide.

The most affordable of this type is called *knock down* (kd) or *ready to assemble* (rta), which you build yourself—easier said than done, unless you're good at reading instructions and handy with a hammer. What you gain in immediate satisfaction with ready-to-assemble cabinets, however, you may give up in lasting quality. Because the boxes aren't glued or put together in a factory setting, they may sag sooner than you'd like. Over time, the particleboard interiors tend to crumble and disintegrate.

A rung up the ready-made ladder, in terms of cost and quality, is the so-called stock option. Stock, or preassembled, cabinets are typically made of melamine (a plastic) or particleboard with laminate or wood veneer fronts. They are available in a slightly wider range of sizes and finishes than the knock-down variety. While they're called *stock,* the cabinets, which you buy at home improvement and kitchen stores, are not always *in* stock. You often wait two to four weeks for delivery. If stock cabinets are the best option for your budget but you're lusting after

TRADE TIP

No matter where you shop, when it comes to cost, you can count on certain givens. Raised panels are more expensive than recessed. Inset doors with exposed hinges are pricier than the frameless type with hidden hinges (exposed hinges require greater detailing because they must fit precisely with the exposed frame, whereas interior hinges are hidden and inherently more adjustable). Drawers are more costly than doors. Cabinets that are glazed run more than those that are painted. Cherry is steeper in price than oak. Glass doors are a significant upcharge.

TRADE TIP

Here's a quick way to judge a cabinet's quality: Look at the drawer, which must be sturdy and well crafted because it takes the brunt of kitchen activity—slams, bangs, dings, and so on. Fortunately, drawer construction is easy to check. Look for rigid wood on the front and sides and plywood on the bottom (far better than the flimsier particleboard). Also check for joints that are dovetailed or doweled rather than those held together by staples and glue. Yet another way to judge a drawer, of course, is to open and close it. The better the mechanism (and there are some top-notch types out there, such as the Blum motion self-closing glide), the smoother the action and the nicer the overall feel.

FIELD NOTE

If you had told me when I first moved into my house fifteen years ago that I would still have the previous owner's kitchen cabinets, I would have said you were crazy. No way. My previous kitchen was on the cover of *House Beautiful*—twice. The custom claret Viking range was even incorporated into Viking's color line. But that was then. . . .

We moved to a larger home in a town with top-notch public schools (key for our four children)—and sky-high property values and taxes. There wasn't much room left in the budget for a kitchen renovation. An initial estimate ran nearly $40,000 for the cabinets alone.

The existing cabinets, with arched fronts in the tombstone style, were killing me. The oak grain was too busy for my taste, and there were none of today's wonderful interior storage amenities like cutlery dividers, pull-out trash and recycling bins, or roll-out shelves in the base cabinets. To add insult to injury, instead of the standard soffit above the cabinets, mine had an actual roof, a sloped one at that, with cedar shingles. There was no choice, financially, but to work with what was there.

We had three days between closing and the start of school to get the kitchen into shape. I called it our kamikaze weekend. Workers swarmed the kitchen. We removed the cabinet roof and exposed the soffit. We had the doors and drawers laminated together so they would pull out as one unit and had their interiors retrofitted with recycling centers, cutlery dividers, and tray storage, all fabricated on site and installed that same weekend. Finally, the busy-looking cabinets were given an overcoat of ebony stain to obscure the pattern of the oak and downplay the tombstone design of the doors.

Fifteen years later, we have done many upgrades to the kitchen—new countertops, appliances, windows, French doors, lighting, moldings, sinks, and backsplashes. In the end, however, between footing the bills for college, law school, and a wedding, we never did get new cabinets. Not yet, anyway.

better design options, think about a mix-and-match approach. Use knock-down or stock cabinets for perimeter cabinetry, which often recedes into the background, and splurge on something that makes a bigger impression, like a customized island, which you see from all four sides. Crown the island with a different countertop, perhaps a stone, and that's what people will notice.

Once you venture into the custom realm, either semi or full, the quality goes up—and there's a greater variety of choices. Semi-custom cabinets are usually ordered from a kitchen showroom, which in turn orders them from a regional or national factory, where the state-of-the-art machinery allows for precise carpentry and flawless finishes. With semi-custom work, you have a range of styles to pick from—as many as thirty door types, for example, along with the opportunity to modify the details: raised, recessed, or ribbed glass-front doors, bead-board accents, moldings, and more. You also get a broader choice of dimension. The width and height of the cabinets are, however, flexible to within 3-inch increments only. Therein lies a potential problem: You can end up with small gaps between the cabinets and the walls or neighboring appliances, which have to be bridged with filler pieces. While these strips are made from the same material as the cabinets and

TRADE TIP

Keep in mind that your cabinet delivery timeline
starts from the moment you sign off on the
final set of design drawings. If you make any
changes—such as switching that triple bank of
drawers to a single drawer and door—then your
cabinetmaker goes back to the drawing board
and your cabinets go to the back of the produc-
tion line.

stained or painted to match, they can still create a patched
look. It's a good idea to ask how many filler pieces your job
will require and where they'll be placed. You may want to
tweak the layout to allow for a flusher fit.

Full custom cabinetry, which costs at least 25 percent
more than semi-custom, is like couture—tailored to your
exact wishes and needs. Made-to-order cabinets are just
that: You can specify the size and shape, the wood
species, and the interior configuration. If you have an
unusual request that's outside of a cabinetmaker's reper-
toire—for an intricate Ionic column on an island, let's
say—you may to have shop around for a specialty craftsman who has the appropriate routers and drill bits. The
precision involved with custom work takes time, of
course; you can't expect delivery for at least a couple of
months, and most likely more.

The appeal of full custom—that it imposes few, if any,
limitations on your imagination—can be the very thing
that makes novice renovators nervous. To veteran renovators, who are comfortable with making decisions and have
the advantage of hindsight, the blank slate can be liberating. But for people given to wavering or self-doubt, the
prospect of making each and every choice can be daunting.
These renovators should either stay with semi-custom or
tap someone with experience for field-narrowing advice.

Wherever you fall on the cabinet continuum, from
knock-down to full-out custom, I suggest you have your

overall kitchen plans in hand—literally—before you shop or buy. That means both the kitchen floor plan (drawn to scale by you or, better yet, the architect) and the specs for all appliances (which will affect the dimensions of the cabinets). Based on those drawings, the cabinetmaker or kitchen showroom rep should be able to give you a price range, if not the exact price, which is determined once you select the finish and layer in the interior amenities—and once he or she knows you're serious about your new kitchen and not just window-shopping. As soon as you put down a deposit, ask to see cabinetry elevations—a wall's-eye view. In the case of custom work, which is typically sold directly to customers by cabinetmakers or millwork shops, it makes sense to check references and see finished work in the form of the kitchens of two or three happy customers.

The Anatomy of a Cabinet

As simple as a cabinet sounds, it is actually made up of several parts. The inside box, the carcass, is an open-faced cube, cut from one of three types of material. The top in quality is furniture-grade plywood. A close second-best is medium-density fiberboard (MDF), which is coated in polyester, so it's sturdy and moisture-resistant—more so even than plywood. The least expensive (and least desirable) is particleboard—basically compressed sawdust, which can look fine initially but doesn't hold up over time.

The front piece—the door of the cabinet or the front panel of a drawer—is then attached to the carcass. And here's where you have a decision to make that will greatly influence the look of your kitchen: Will your doors and drawers be *framed* or *frameless?*

With the more traditional, framed type, also known as *face-framed,* the cabinet door or drawer is mounted on a flat piece (the frame) that has been applied to the face of the box with the hinges proudly on view. The door or drawers may sit fully within the frame or partially overlay it. Either way, a visual frame is created—a historically accurate effect and a nod to the way cabinets were

made before machinery. Precise fit is essential, or the doors and drawers won't line up and close properly. This careful craftsmanship takes time, which accounts for the slightly higher price of this type of cabinetry.

The framed door carries with it a different kind of cost, too: You sacrifice some of the interior room; the frame compromises the size of the cabinets, making doors and drawers as much as 1 or 2 inches smaller, depending on the size of the frame. Another detail to consider: If your plan calls for double-width cabinets (over 36 inches wide), you will end up with a center rail that restricts accessibility, meaning you'll have to reach around the rail to put away pots, for instance. One final caveat: A multitude of framed doors—rectangles within rectangles and squares within squares—can make for a busy-looking space, particularly if the kitchen is on the small side.

FIELD NOTE

When it comes to cabinet fillers, I've had my fill. My first filler experience was with the kitchen I designed for my parents when they moved from their family-raising home to a cottage. Downsizing meant sandwiching themselves and a good portion of their kitchen paraphernalia (my parents weren't about to downsize their frequent entertaining) into the much smaller space. The new compact kitchen maximized every linear inch and worked without a hitch—that is, until my mother tried to empty the icemaker. The freezer door handle hit the protruding side wall, not a problem for ordinary usage but an impediment when trying to pull out the ice drawer. To solve the problem, I had a recess notched into the adjacent Sheetrock wall to allow for ice unloading.

Years later, I replaced my ancient 27-inch-wide wall ovens with spanking new 30-inch convection ovens. To make room, I cut some of the fill from the existing cabinets. All worked wonderfully well until Thanksgiving, when both ovens were in full swing. It was then that I noticed I couldn't fully open the lower oven; it was inhibited by a small projecting knob on the radiator on the perpendicular wall. Oops. As the upper oven is completely accessible and the lower oven accessible except for that last inch, we live with it.

CABINETRY THROUGH THE AGES:
A STYLE TIMELINE

THE FIFTIES. This is the era of simple painted wood boxes or metal cabinets (no raised panels or moldings yet) with stainless-steel handles (no knobs yet, either!).

THE SIXTIES. Formica comes to the forefront. Like the famous line in *The Graduate,* the one word is *plastics.* Innovation and ease of maintenance drive the Formica fad. Kitchens are still just for cooking.

THE SEVENTIES. Cabinets become more furniture-like with paneling, trims, molding, and bead detailing added to the flat panel styles. Raised paneling presents a new-old decorative look. Natural woods, particularly oak, encourage homeowners to go with the grain. Antique brass hardware replaces chrome. Arch-topped styles (called *tombstone*) are all the rage.

THE EIGHTIES. The wood grains lighten up with pickling and new, pale limed oaks. This is the heyday of white-painted raised-panel cabinets with shiny brass hardware. New interior amenities—cutlery dividers, knife slots, spice doors, corner swivels—become de rigueur.

THE NINETIES. Cherry cabinets sweep the scene in the early 1990s, along with walnut and quarter-sawn oak in the latter part of the decade. Cabinets grow taller and more elaborate, with decorative flourishes such as columns and embossed moldings. The appetite for all things big grows—supersized bowls, oversized plates, giant mugs—creating the need for more cabinet space.

THE HERE AND NOW. It's back to a cleaner look in shape and detail, while the finishes grow warmer and more sophisticated. Tighter-grained, darker woods emerge, along with exotic species (zebra, African mahogany). Whites are softer and warmer, often glazed. Finishes are frequently mixed—natural wood paired with a painted island, for example. A welcome development: Cabinetmakers design ancillary furniture pieces or cabinetry to make room for auxiliary appliances such as microwaves and cappuccino makers. Stainless-steel cabinets make a comeback. What goes around comes around. . . .

TRADE TIP

If you expect your cabinets to take a beating—doors being banged shut constantly or leaned upon while their contents are being inspected—think about using cup hinges, most commonly available on frameless cabinets. These hinges, also known as *C*-hinges, are easy to adjust on both the vertical and horizontal plane should a door sag out of alignment.

The other choice in basic construction is the frameless cabinet, also called *full overlay*—a style popularized in midcentury Europe that still looks fresh and relevant. Frameless cabinets, in which the door covers the entire face of the box, are slightly less expensive to make and easier to install and later adjust. There's no visible space between the doors and drawers, with no posts or rails interrupting the design, and the hinges are hidden within. This makes for a clean-looking exterior—certainly an advantage, from a minimalist's viewpoint. That doesn't mean, however, that all frameless doors must be strictly contemporary in design. You can, with help from a cooperative semi-custom showroom or cabinetmaker, combine a frameless construction with a more traditional or decorative set of drawers and doors—for some renovators, a best-of-both-worlds scenario.

Sizing Up the Cabinets

With the style of construction established, it's time to map out the placement of the cabinetry. Step back and take stock of what kind of storage you can accommodate once your appliances are chosen—and, presumably, immovably established. Think about *all* of it, the whole mountain of what you'll need to stow in your kitchen: the kids' sippy cups, the coffee mugs, trays, mixing bowls, Tupperware, plastic bags, cloth napkins, lunch bags, foils, pot lids, cereals . . . to say nothing of multiple sets of cutlery and dinnerware.

[TOP] A PLAN FOR PLACEMENT: WHEN DECIDING WHAT GOES INTO WHAT DRAWER, CONSIDER HOW AND WHERE YOU'LL BE USING EACH ITEM. PUT THE SANDWICH BAGS CLOSE TO WHERE YOU MAKE THE KIDS' LUNCHES, THE STRAWS BESIDE THE CUPS, AND THE NAPKINS AND PLACE MATS NEAR THE TABLE.

[ABOVE] FULL OVERLAY WALNUT DOORS—NO VISIBLE HINGES, NO UNNECESSARY FILL PIECES—LET THE WARM WOOD GRAIN BE THE STANDOUT.

Technical terms are bandied about as if you know what the professionals are talking about. To be in the thick of kitchen remodeling, you need to know all the right words, or you may end up with some surprises. If you don't know, *ask*.

SOFFIT STARTER. A flat piece of cabinetry wood, topped by a row of crown molding, that brings the line of your cabinets up to the ceiling. Some renovators use multiple rows of molding over a soffit to meet a high ceiling.

C-HINGE. A European-style concealed heavy-duty hinge. Bulky and cumbersome looking but sturdy and easy to adjust.

AFTERMARKET OR AFTERLIFE. The term the kitchen industry uses for storage amenities you can layer into your cabinets after they are installed. You can order pull-out trash and recycling bins, undersink storage compartments, and wooden peg systems from a variety of firms, including sleek and well-made European options.

SCRIBES OR FILLERS. Pieces that are easily planed to fill gaps between two cabinets (fillers) or between a cabinet and a wall (scribes) to make cabinets appear flush and fill in the gaps. None of us live in a plumb-level world, let alone home.

TOE KICK OR KICKSPACE. A recess at the bottom of a base cabinet that provides room for your toes so you can work up close and personal at your countertop. Toe kicks are a must on all lower cabinets. European models have a high 6-inch to 9-inch toe kick compared to the 4 to 4½ inches of American designs.

Organize your cabinet's contents logically: Store things where they'll most likely be used, not just where they happen to fit. Point-of-use storage is what makes your kitchen work for you. You might, for example, want your place mats in a cabinet near your table and your spices on a cool, dry shelf that's close to the oven (but not so close they get hot and dried out). If you're the type who can never remember where you put the corkscrew, this is the time to plan for a drawer near the wine cooler. By the same token, you don't want your cutlery drawer or shelf for glassware across the room from the dishwasher. To my mind, there's only one upper cabinet that is indispensable: the one into which you unload the dishwasher contents. Unloading the dishwasher is, after all, an unending chore; having drawers and cabinets close at hand makes it a little less onerous.

The Details of Dimensions

Once you've figured out the overall placement, it's time to get into the minutiae of measurements. Widthwise, you'll usually have a range of choices, from 9 inches up to 48. In my experience, fewer, wider cabinets make more sense than many narrow ones. I like to be able to open a pair of large cabinet doors and take a full inventory rather than checking behind door A, door B, and back to door A. More width also makes getting things out and putting things away easier; you don't have that constant rejiggering to make your mugs fit with your juice glasses. On the other hand, a wide door swing can be awkward in a cramped space; make certain you won't need to duck or bob to avoid getting thwacked in the face.

The wider-is-better advice generally holds for drawers, which can be up to 36 inches wide but are typically specified narrower. A cutlery drawer should be at least 21 inches wide—and as much as 27 inches—to make room for place settings and flatware accoutrements. If you have a choice between more drawers and more cabinets, I usually vote for drawers. After all, you slide them open in a single motion, and cabinets with pull-outs inside, while handy, are a two-step operation: open the doors, pull out the drawer. You also have to remember to open the doors all the way—to a full 90 degrees—otherwise, the inside of your door will be pockmarked with dings. That said, cabinets with pull-out shelves have one distinct advantage: They're adjustable, meaning they can accommodate both tall pots and small appliances with ease.

Cabinets that are too small have a limited role, unless they're designated for certain specific uses, such as vertical tray storage or a pull-out pantry. In my own kitchen, for instance, I had a ridiculously small 9-inch cabinet space that I turned into a pull-out mini-pantry on glides. Two narrow shelves were inserted to house teas, coffees, jams, and soup cans, transforming the space from dead air into a cabinet used daily.

How about height? Upper cabinets have grown, in part to acknowledge taller ceiling heights in new construction, in part to frame our new 7-foot fridges, and in part to banish that grease collector, the soffit (the so-called closed soffit, where the Sheetrock comes down to meet upper cabinets, is common in older homes). In fact, the height of upper cabinetry has increased an average of 1 foot over the last decade or two, from 30 inches to between 36 and 48 inches.

While building tall is logical from a practical and visual sense—to make use of wasted or dead space—it adds to the construction cost. The differential between a 36-inch and a 42-inch cabinet is negligible, but a 48-inch cabinet generally requires a hefty upcharge. And if you're not a professional basketball player, you have to ask yourself if you'll even be able to reach the extra storage space without a stepstool.

In terms of stability, too, there is a limit to how high something can be built. If you need an especially tall door—taller than 60 inches for a pantry unit, for instance—consider hinging two doors together to work as one; otherwise, you risk having a cabinet door that will torque or twist out of alignment over time. Stacked cabinets, also called scullery cabinets, are another way to take advantage of vertical space. When done artfully, with an eye to proportion, stacked cabinets can become a handsome kitchen focal point.

Of the three cabinet dimensions, depth, unfortunately, hasn't budged. It is a pet peeve of mine that cabinets are anachronistically

built to the same depth as a century ago! The typical upper cabinet yields 11 or 12 inches of interior space—not large enough for a microwave, a panini-maker, or most platters. The explanation for this lack of depth likely lies in the fact that sheet goods (the material out of which we make our cabinets) come in standard 4-foot increments. It's logical, then, that manufacturers would make base cabinets 24 inches and upper cabinets 12 inches. To create deeper cabinets means a lot of waste and, hence, higher cost. A handful of cabinet manufacturers will construct cabinets that are a few critical inches deeper—for an upcharge, of course.

As for the lower cabinets, the typical depth of 24 inches is usually more than adequate in terms of storage. But deep lower cabinets translate into additional counter space—and isn't that something we could all use a bit more of? With all the appliances, breadboxes, and coffeemakers crowding the countertops, base cabinets should ideally be 3 inches deeper—27 inches instead of 24. Fortunately, you can fake the effect by having standard (that is, economical) base cabinets shimmed out from the wall a bit. Voilà! A deeper countertop.

Breaking the Plane

As important as measuring to fit is when it comes to kitchen cabinetry, there are definitely times it's worth thinking outside the box. Consider, for example, intentionally breaching all those horizontal lines created by the upper and lower cabinets by having one portion of upper cabinets migrate down and sit right on the countertop. This cupboard effect, reminiscent of an English or Welsh cabinet, breaks up a vast expanse of countertop with style—and, to my eye, always looks handsome and smart.

[OPPOSITE, ABOVE] A TALL AND SKINNY PULLOUT CABINET FOR FOOD STORAGE IS ABSOLUTELY THE BEST WAY TO MAXIMIZE A NARROW SPACE. THIS ONE HAS WIRE SHELVING AND OPEN SIDES TO TAKE ADVANTAGE OF EVERY AVAILABLE INCH. A WORD OF CAUTION: WHEN THESE STORAGE UNITS GET TOO WIDE, THEY CAN BECOME UNWIELDY TO PULL IN AND OUT—18 INCHES SHOULD BE THE MAX.

[OPPOSITE, BELOW] SIDE-FACING (AS OPPOSED TO STANDARD OUTWARD-FACING), CABINET DOORS CAN BE AWKWARD TO OPEN. A CLEVER SOLUTION: A BIFOLD DOOR, HINGED IN THE CENTER, MAKES THE CABINET'S CONTENTS FAR EASIER TO ACCESS.

[ABOVE LEFT] A TWO-IN-ONE BREAD DRAWER TRICK: A CUTTING BOARD SITS ON TOP OF A DEEP STORAGE SPACE IN THE FORM OF A LUCITE BOX. BOTH COMPONENTS LIFT OUT EASILY FOR CLEANING.

[ABOVE RIGHT] TO AVOID CLUTTER ON THE COUNTER, THIS FAMILY HAD THE CONTRACTOR NOTCH OUT SPACE BETWEEN THE WALL STUDS, CREATING AN APPLIANCE NICHE, OR A "PORTE COCHERE"—A CHIC ALTERNATIVE TO THE TYPICAL APPLIANCE GARAGE WITH DOORS.

[ABOVE LEFT] A DEEP CORNER CABINET USUALLY MEANS DEAD SPACE. A SO-CALLED MAGIC CORNER PROVIDES A SHELVING SYSTEM THAT RESOLVES THE PROBLEM. WHEN YOU OPEN THE DOOR, THE SHELF AND ALL ITS CONTENTS ARE PULLED FORWARD FOR BETTER VIEWING AND ACCESS.

[ABOVE RIGHT] APPLIANCE GARAGES KEEP SMALL APPLIANCES UNDER COVER AND OUT OF SIGHT, BUT OFTEN THEIR DOORS WREAK CREATIVE HAVOC ON THE COUNTER. ROLLTOP DOORS HAVE A HABIT OF JAMMING, AND SWING-OUT TYPES CAN KNOCK THINGS OVER. THE BETTER SOLUTION: A FLIP-UP DOOR.

TRADE TIP

Regardless of the overall altitude, I recommend ordering additional shelves for upper cabinetry. Often, interior shelves are spaced equidistantly, allowing much more room than the average kitchen needs for diminutive juice glasses or even your basic coffee cup. Odds are you'll have room to insert an extra shelf (or two) to increase interior storage.

You can do a variation on this theme by pulling just the base cabinets forward and perhaps detailing them with furniture elements, such as columns or decorative feet. That projection of the base cabinets not only interrupts the tedium of a straight run of cabinetry but also offers the opportunity to extend the countertop. The extra counter depth makes a great port for a pro-style range but is less useful at the sink, where I prefer to see a straight run of countertop and where the extra inches in front make the sink less accessible.

Along the same lines, identify a spot for a counter-height kitchen desk or message center, which can be made from the same material as the cabinetry. You don't need to dedicate a lot of room for this type of desk. I find most clients like to simply scoot up a stool and perch at the counter, but don't shortchange yourself, either. Think of your needs in all dimensions: horizontally (for a laptop, desktop supplies), vertically (a bulletin board, open cookbook shelving), and under-counter (file drawers for directories, class lists). For more on kitchen office options, see pages 201–202 in the "Auxiliary Spaces" chapter.

Inside the Box:
Storage Tricks and Turns

Tricking out the interior of a cabinet with storage solutions is a big part of the appeal of new cabinetry. But you don't necessarily have to wait for a complete kitchen redo to put some of these ideas to use. Many cabinets can be retrofitted with roll-outs, swivels, and spice racks. The key is separating the good from the bad or flimsy.

- The stock appliance garages offered by cabinetmakers can sometimes come up short. My customers complain that things never fit exactly right and they have to pull everything out to get anything in. Plus, the tambour-type rolling doors that are often installed have a habit of getting stuck, especially in warm or sticky weather. Rather than simply accept what's offered off the shelf, measure whatever you want to hide from view and specify that the garage-style cabinet use a standard swinging or flip-up door.

- Lazy Susans or the more aptly named super Susans make dead and deep corner space accessible—a good thing indeed. The potential problem is that stock Susans are often flimsy little plastic shelves with a center post, which cramps storage. They wobble and fall apart. Look for a sturdy wooden Susan with no center post, and one that allows you to pull or rotate one shelf at a time without turning the entire unit.

- So-called magic corners are another way to provide access to corner cabinets. As the door opens, an attached shelf-storage unit pulls forward, exposing a second shelf-storage unit from the recesses of the corner. *Note:* You need at least 39 inches along a flat wall for a magic corner to work (versus 36 inches for a typical lazy Susan).

- A fold-down mixer shelf is a spring-loaded shelf that actually swings up and out of a bottom cabinet, ready to deliver your electric mixer or food processor to counter height. Unfortunately, the heavy mixers you want to use these shelves for don't always clear the front of the cabinet frame. It's probably smarter to save the expense of the custom-design swing shelf and sit the mixer on a regular shelf or the counter.

- A singularly bad idea: a tilt-out drawer under the sink to stow damp sponges. Let's see, bacteria-laden items in a small, airless compartment. Can you say rot? mildew? Just leave your sponge out on the sink and call it a day.

- While nothing beats the convenience of a bank of drawers, pull-out shelves are a close second. You can fit any standard cabinet with pull-out or roll-out shelves. Just train yourself to open the doors all the way out, a full 90 degrees, so the inside of the doors don't accumulate countless dings where the roll-outs hit.

[TOP] DRAWERS ARE IDEALLY SUITED FOR SPICE STORAGE. JUST THE RIGHT DEPTH AND HEIGHT, AND EVERYTHING IS VISIBLE.

[ABOVE] IF THE CONTRACTOR AND THE CABINETMAKER ARE LONG GONE, YOU CAN STILL ADD YOUR OWN STORAGE AMENITIES—THERE ARE COUNTLESS CHOICES AT HOME STORES. CASE IN POINT: THESE SMALL LAZY SUSANS THAT ARE IDEAL FOR SPICES. NO NEED TO RUMMAGE AROUND TO SEE WHAT'S HIDDEN IN THE BACK OF THE CABINET.

Don't add too many decorative trim pieces. Acanthus leaves, grapevines, twisted turn columns, pilasters, triple-crown moldings, and full-height columns that pull out as pantries add up to too much. The kitchen already has a *lot* of stuff: fridge, microwave, range, recycling bins. It really doesn't need much extra decoration.

Don't get high-gloss reflective cabinet surface finishes unless you want a Windex bottle grafted to your cleaning hand.

Do without rather than cheapen out. Skip ordering bells and whistles for the interior and go for top quality on the cabinets you'll use every day.

Do oversize. Bigger is almost always better; opt for one bigger cabinet instead of two smaller cabinets.

Do factor in your height and the height of your countertop appliances before deciding where to mount your upper cabinets. Too high, and you may not be able to reach the second shelf, let alone the third. Too low, and your beloved coffeemaker may have to sit in front of the cabinets rather than tucked underneath.

Do subdivide to suit, but don't overdivide (or create too many subdivided drawers). Flatware is your most micro-divided. For cooking cutlery, think more macro.

- Spice drawers consist of multiple rows of angled trays set into a drawer. On the plus side, the drawer props up the jars and makes for easy access and label readings (versus the awkwardness when you stack them in the pantry). On the other hand, not all spice jars fit in neatly, and those that are oversized or undersized wobble around. Should you opt for a spice drawer, remember that cooler locations work better than warmer ones to keep spices fresh and not dried out.

- Knife quivers, or knife blocks, can be built right into a drawer so knives can slip in vertically, blade side down. I much prefer this to the usual options of the knife block that sits on the countertop and takes up space or the magnetic knife-holding strip that hangs on the backsplash. Make sure the insert holds all your knives; minor adjustment may be necessary. An added incentive: When the knives sit in the insert neatly and cleanly, you'll find you'll rarely have to sharpen them.

- Plate peg systems allow you to put plates in a bottom drawer without worrying about them rolling around or nicking or chipping. The idea: A wooden pegboard cut to fit in the bottom of your base cabinet drawer is fitted with adjustable pegs

FIELD NOTE

Two seemingly similar knobs, both in simple stainless steel, can feel remarkably different in hand. Angela Edwards and her husband, Dave, were independently drawn to the same knob—a sleek flat-back model. When I screwed the knob into their cabinet door and asked them to open it, they both nixed the choice. The flat-back was just too close to the cabinet to pull comfortably. The runner-up choice was a slightly bigger knob with a rounded back that made grasping much easier—a reminder that as good as hardware looks, its primary job is to function.

MIXED GRAINS: IN AN OLD HOME WITH THE ORIGINAL OLD BEAMS AND RUSTIC WIDE-PLANKED WALLS, WALNUT CABINETS, WITH THEIR CONSISTENT GRAIN, MAKE FOR AN UNDERSTATED COMPLEMENT. A BUSIER GRAIN WOULD HAVE COMPETED WITH THE COUNTRY PLANKS.

that act as a framework to hold plates in place. Most pegs are 4 to 6 inches tall, round or triangular, and with a concave cutout on the hypotenuse to hug the dishes. Any drawer or pull-out can be fitted with a peg system—a particular boon for those who store plates in base cabinets. You can order these with your cabinetry or retrofit existing cabinets with specially designed pegs and pegboards (cleats on the pegboard allow room for the pegs to be inserted).

- Twin bins are the single best cabinet storage invention—back-to-back garbage bins, one for trash, the other for recycling, that slide into a single base unit. You need at least an 18-inch-wide frameless cabinet to hold the bins; you need at least a 21-inch-wide framed cabinet. This cabinet usually comes with an upper drawer you can use for garbage bags or dish towels—not food, for obvious reasons.

- If you have just a bit of space—as few as 9 inches—consider a pull-out pantry as an efficient and effective option. It has room enough for tea, jams, and some canned goods.

- Pass on the elaborate pantry systems with racks and swivels that are mounted on the back of doors; they are simply too cumbersome. To reach that can of soup on the back shelf, you have to open a door and swing out a rack with hundreds of pounds of stuff loaded on it. Simpler is better. Take that same space, install five roll-out shelves inside, and you've got what one client calls her Costco closet—inexpensive, accessible storage for bulk items.

Material Gains

As important as the other cabinet decisions are, it's unlikely someone will walk into your kitchen and think, "Wow, that's really amazing frameless construction." It's the finish—the wood or laminate, the color or stain—that makes the most immediate impression.

Most people choose wood, probably because it represents quality, adds visual warmth, and comes in many options. The two most requested species, cherry and maple, are also the hardest-wearing. Cherry is, of course, reddish in tone, and it tends to darken dramatically with age. For that reason, it's critical that cherry be finished properly with a sealant that protects it from UV light; otherwise it can look gloomy after a few years. Even with a sealant, cherry will darken, albeit more gradually. For that reason, some renovators prefer to stain the wood dark from the get-go—and, in fact, cherry takes rich stains such as mahogany exceptionally well.

On the other hand, maple starts off light in color and tends to look best when it stays that way. Deep stain looks muddy over maple's clear grain. That's not to say maple can't be effectively stained—either a rich brown or a translucent color—but the quality of the finish is key. Manufacturers tend to tout their method as best (implying the more steps, the better), but the truth is, any process that involves at least seven steps (sanding, baking, sanding, baking, etc.) is more than adequate. Maple's flat grain also makes it an ideal base for a painted finish.

Renovators also frequently opt for walnut or mahogany for their cabinetry. Both are hard, dark woods, brown in color, although mahogany can have a burgundy cast. Alder, a versatile western wood that can be stained a variety of ways, is also gaining ground and has the distinct advantage of costing an average of 40 percent less than cherry.

The wood family includes many other far-flung cousins. Quartersawn white oak is a particular favorite of mine. It doesn't cathedral like regular oak, creating vivid grains that peak repeatedly like a cathedral's spire. Instead, quartersawn oak has a distinctive straight grain with ray flecks; it is the hallmark of the Arts and Crafts look. Knotty cherry, which has the same color and hardness as regular cherry, has knots and pinholes for a rustic charm. Chestnut and pecky cypress have a highly prized wormy look. For a more sophisticated statement, curly maple and bird's-eye maple flaunt an overt grain.

[OPPOSITE] EARLY KITCHENS WEREN'T OUTFITTED LIKE TODAY'S KITCHENS— RATHER, THEY GREW. THEY OFTEN FEATURED MULTIPLE SURFACES SUCH AS MARBLE-TOPPED PREP TABLES AND GLASS-DOORED PANTRY CABINETS.

[BELOW] WHEN A KITCHEN HAS A LOT OF WOOD ALREADY, CONSIDER ADDING A LITTLE COLOR IN THE FORM OF A PIECE OF FURNITURE. HERE, A BARN-RED HUTCH—WITH AN ARTFUL DISPLAY OF MAJOLICA—IS WARM YET ENLIVENING.

When it comes to top-finishing any natural grain, I recommend either a matte or a satin finish; both are low-sheen and easier to maintain than contemporary high-gloss, which shows every ding. Some homeowners are reluctant to treat their brand-new wood, afraid they will change its character with a varnish. Actually, leaving the wood unfinished will allow it to change without a doubt. Left untreated, wood darkens over time—and not always gracefully. Lighter woods (maple, birch, pine) tend to get more yellow, while darker woods darken dramatically.

Accents: Exotics, Stainless, and Glass

Traditional wood—oak, maple, cherry, birch, walnut, or mahogany—is the traditional choice for cabinets. There are times (and spaces), however, that call for something more unusual. Exotic woods, such as wenge and zebrawood, are in vogue as a border or insert to accent more typical grains. In the case of these exotics, veneer actually makes more sense than solid wood, both from a cost standpoint and to ensure that the somewhat delicate woods have enough dimensional stability. A veneer applied over unwavering MDF guarantees that the glamorous woods will stay on the straight and narrow without cupping. (Veneer is recommended in other circumstances as well, such as when you have an oversized door.)

To add variety to a sea of wooden cabinetry, some homeowners are flashing a bit of stainless steel as an insert in a wooden frame or as a feature on an island. While stainless can make for a beautiful accent in a contemporary kitchen, you have to think about upkeep. Stainless steel, although eminently stylish and quite at home in a minimalist, modern kitchen, is a trade-off. The shiny surface, which is noisy and cold to the touch, is soft enough to dent when something slams into it. Further, fingerprints show and water immediately beads on the surface, practically requiring a squeegee to keep it dry. When I see a stainless-steel kitchen, I wonder if the owners are cooks. If they are, they must also be clean freaks! Brushed aluminum is another metallic option—one that costs a bit more but camouflages scratches better than stainless.

Glass doors are a stylish way to break up a long run of solid upper cabinetry. They can be ordered with a single windowpane, Gothic-style arches, diamonds, or multiple mullions. If you're enamored of mullions, I encourage you to order true individual panes of glass divided by wooden mullions rather than the snap-in grills, which are less expensive but flimsy and fake-looking.

Or, perhaps better yet, eliminate mullions altogether. If the adjustable horizontal shelves don't align precisely with the fixed horizontal mullions—

TRADE TIP

When shopping for glass-fronted cabinets, make sure the glass sits securely within the cabinet door frame. Open and close the door a few times, checking for rattling or shaking. The more solid the glass feels, the less chance it will crack or shatter later with an unexpected slam.

[OPPOSITE] THIRTY-INCH-HIGH CABINETS ARE WOEFULLY SHORT BY TODAY'S STANDARDS. DESIGNER KRISTIINA RATIA COMPENSATES FOR THEIR SHORT STATURE BY PUTTING THE SOFFIT ABOVE TO GOOD USE AS AD HOC STORAGE FOR HER COLLECTION OF RUSSIAN COPPER POTS.

and to maximize interior dish storage, they often don't—then the horizontals will look doubled-up and too stripy. And unless your doors are very wide, a vertical mullion makes the panes too small and Disneyesque. The door rails themselves give the look of vertical lines, and the interior shelves serve as the horizontal lines.

You can also opt to have the glass itself be a decorative feature. Seeded glass (deliberately pebbly and wavy) or ribbed glass (clean, contemporary, and linear) are two good-looking options. Whatever the finishing detail, you want to use glass judiciously. After all, it becomes a window to the cabinet's contents. While a well-arranged display of creamware is appealing, no one really wants to see an open box of Oreos.

Paints and Glazes

While some people like the natural look of stained wood or the sleek effect of stainless, others are partial to a painted finish. If you choose to go the painted route, be sure the underlying cabinetry is up to the task. Maple and poplar cabinets take paint well, as do certain high-quality MDF cabinets, which have the benefit of not separating with swings of humidity over time. Wood painted a light color tends to show tiny dark lines as the wood expands and contracts over time wherever the wood strips are joined (the effect is pleasingly authentic to some, unsightly to others). In terms of hue, white is a timeless choice, but it's not the only one: Shades of neutrals, like buttercream or putty, have a scullery-like appeal; blues, blacks, or greens can make handsome

accents for an island. With any painted finish, application is key. If you want a flawless surface, it's wise to order the cabinet already painted with a factory-applied finish. If you plan to paint your cabinets yourself or have a professional do them on site, be sure the cabinets are impeccably prepped and use oil-based enamel from a good-quality manufacturer such as Benjamin Moore. The glossy finish not only has an attractive sheen but also is easy to wipe clean.

A subtler way to add translucent color is via glazing. Glazes can be white (think French provincial) or, more commonly, dark, in shades of burnt umber, sienna, charcoal, or pewter, and can be applied over a painted or stained surface. Most glazes are sprayed or brushed on and then wiped off by hand so just a bit of color remains in the crevices. Glazing makes the most sense when you want to highlight moldings or carpentry details, and it adds a three-dimensional shading effect especially suited to a cottage or country look. (A slight variation is called the dry brush look, in which you see streaks and striations.) As for wear, glazing gets mixed reviews: While it's no more or less resistant to scratching than standard paint, a glaze disguises the usual knocks a bit better—a nick looks like just another highlight. Overall, however, decorative glazes are harder to touch up than plain finishes.

GETTING THE DETAILS RIGHT: FOR
THIS PANTRY UNIT, THE OWNER
PAIRED BIN PULLS WITH OLD-
FASHIONED REFRIGERATOR LATCHES
AND HID THE HINGES SO AS NOT TO
DETRACT FROM THE VINTAGE FEEL.

[RIGHT] TURNING A SOW'S EAR INTO A SILK PURSE... FANCIFUL HISTORIC HANDLES WITH TASSELS DRESS UP OLD FORMICA DOORS.

Finishing Features: Moldings, Hinges, and Hardware

Once you've decided on the basic material and finish, you can think about the details of the doors—the woodwork features, the hardware, and the hinges. A word of caution: Don't overembellish. Keep in mind, and in your mind's eye, that once you multiply a detail by a room full of doors and drawers, it can come off as fussy or overdecorated.

The same think-twice advice extends to the base of the cabinets. In an effort to make cabinetry look more furniture-like, some home-owners are adding rounded wood bun feet and carpentry details to base cabinets. A true furniture foot is open to the wall below the cabinet, which is not always practical; think of escaped grapes rolling underneath—not easy to retrieve. A so-called pseudo furniture foot is one that's backed by a toe kick (a base that's recessed just enough to allow room for your toes underneath). For the most part, I think furniture feet should stay on furniture. The exception is on an island or a peninsula—which, when you think about it, resemble furniture to begin with. Adding either a set of feet or a furniture base (meaning a bottom molding that sits on the surface of the cabinet rather than stepping in, like a toe kick) can be a handsome finishing touch. What you don't want is a toe kick on the seating side. It leaves your cabinet base hanging out in the middle of the room, where it tends to look like a puzzle missing the bottom piece.

Moldings, a decorative feature to consider at the joint between the wall and the ceiling, are a way to marry the cabinetry with the ceiling. If your ceilings are on the high side, you may find you've got extra dead space between the top of the cabinets and the ceiling itself that's calling out for masking. One solution is to use a flat piece of matching woodwork (called a soffit starter), ordered as an accessory from the cabinetmaker, to bridge the gap. You can then embellish it with moldings, sometimes in multiples, to meet the ceiling. Again, avoid aggrandizement. I find understated molding offers a more timeless choice than grapevines or acanthus leaves.

Hardware is often called the jewelry of cabinetry, and the metaphor is apt. Good-quality hardware has the decorative power to transform the look of the kitchen, and it is expensive. There is no shortage of choices from which to select—bin pulls, icebox latches, cupboard latches, porcelain knobs, marble knobs, twisted iron handles, whimsical frogs, sea glass flowers—all in finishes such as brass, iron, chrome, wood, pewter, glass, rubber, nickel, hammered copper, cast iron, or rustic oil-rubbed bronze.

Where to start? With your cabinetmaker or cabinet shop, which will undoubtedly offer quite a range. But if you don't see something

[ABOVE AND BELOW] IF THE INSIDES OF YOUR CABINET AREN'T GOING TO MATCH THE EXTERIORS, AS THEY OFTEN DON'T, IT'S A GOOD MOVE TO ORDER AN OVERLAY DOOR OR DRAWER, WHICH ENSURES THAT YOU WON'T CATCH A GLIMPSE OF THE CONTRASTING INTERIOR WHEN THE DRAWER IS SHUT.

[OPPOSITE] MOLDING IN MODERATION: IN A KITCHEN CAPPED WITH A SOFFIT THAT HOUSES AIR CONDITIONING, THE QUESTION WAS WHERE TO RUN THE CROWN MOLDING. WISELY, THE OWNERS CONFINED THE CROWN TO THEIR CABINETRY AND LEFT THE SOFFIT UNADORNED.

you love, not to worry. Countless options are available from sources as familiar as Restoration Hardware and Home Depot, as fashionable as Anthropologie. There are also many websites to browse (a favorite is TopKnobsUSA.com). Unlike with other kitchen essentials, ordering hardware is relatively risk free; you can buy a single sample before committing to a kitchen's worth. This is particularly crucial with pulls and handles. They must accommodate your fingertips easily, or you will always be fumbling with the handle or snagging your nails. Bin pulls, for instance, are remarkably uncomfortable to use on a day-to-day basis for many of my clients—all the more reason to test drive before you buy.

As for the question of knobs or handles, the answer is often both. There's no reason not to vary your hardware if you want, outfitting drawers with knobs and doors with handles, or vice versa. On drawers, the knob or handle is installed dead center. On doors, however, the hardware is typically mounted 6 to 8 inches from the bottom rail to prevent any torque in the door. Before drilling, keep in mind an obvious but frequently overlooked fact: The hole will always be the hole. On the plus side, this means swapping one knob for another is a simple matter. To continue the jewelry analogy, it's as easy as slipping a new pair of pierced earrings into existing holes. Handles are trickier. As handles and pulls have center-to-center dimensions, a change in handles means you will either need to scour the market for handles with the same precise dimensions or resign yourself to plugging and patching the previous holes.

With small details such as knobs and handles, I think bigger is generally better. Look for a knob that is about 1½ inches in diameter. Each ¼ inch makes a meaningful difference. Knobs that are smaller than 1¼ inches look too diminutive; after all, our cabinets have grown to 48 inches and taller. Handles or pulls should be at least 3 inches, as measured by their inside dimensions (the underside of the handle) and can be 6 inches or even longer. Oversized handles, in the 8- or 10-inch range—all the way to 24 inches tall—are especially stylish-looking on stripped-down slab-front cabinetry, and they have the advantage of being easy to grasp. A possible downside, down the road: It will be hard to swap these large handles out for a new look when the oversized handle trend fades. Sure, you can change your cabinet hardware anytime—provided you use the existing holes. Otherwise, even with an expertly applied patch, in all likelihood the finish will never match.

Hinges play second fiddle to knobs and pulls, but they're critical to function; after all, your cabinets couldn't open without them. The *C*-hinge works beautifully in a frameless cabinet. Butt hinges are more traditional and also visible. The charm comes in the form of finials; balls or urns are classic choices.

Given the tendency to mix and match surfaces throughout the kitchen, it's no surprise that hardware offers another decorative fusion opportunity. Just beware of overmixing, or your kitchen will look like a fashion don't. Why not go simple and straightforward for the perimeter cabinets, then take a more whimsical, elegant, or extravagant turn front and center for the pièce de résistance island? The ever-exuberant Raymond Waites chose coral-shaped hardware fashioned from iron for his zebrawood-trimmed island—an inspired combination.

The Surfaces

Inch for inch, the surfaces in a kitchen account for the greatest visual impact of the space. Countertops, floors, and backsplashes carry the color, pattern, and texture, and they create the overall decorative tone. A wood countertop, for instance, creates a different mood than one of stainless steel; a white-tiled floor has a different character than one of green slate. While a new kitchen or a major renovation usually involves every surface in the space, even the refurbishing of a single surface can give a kitchen a lift. A new piece of marble can instantly update and upgrade a tired-looking island. Refinishing a worn oak floor with a rich cherry stain can offer a welcome change of pace.

Because surfaces constitute so much, well, surface area, it's a good idea to consider how the individual materials and colors and patterns will interact with each other—as well as with the cabinetry and appliances—to create a whole. You may fall in love with one element, such as a certain colorful backsplash tile, without taking into account how it will jibe with the expanse of a patterned floor or a run of speckled countertop. Step back and imagine the combined effect of the different surfaces, considering the floor in tandem with the countertops and backsplash. You don't need to choose all of the various elements in the same material or color—in fact, how monotonous might that look?—but they need to work together in the big picture.

More than just visually engaging, surfaces need to be practical, strong, and resilient; they need to stand up to wear and tear. These are the materials that you chop, slice, and dice on, that you spill or splatter over. Those that can take the proverbial heat will end up serving you and your kitchen well.

Counter Culture

Stone, wood, stainless steel, or synthetic—countertops are long on choices, whether you're after a look that's warm and inviting or cool and edgy. Or both. There's no reason to limit yourself to one type of counter within the kitchen. After all, the overall footprint of a kitchen has grown by 50 percent in the last fifteen years while, at the same time, layouts have become less proscribed. Conventions are changing—we're mixing and matching cabinetry finishes; we're buying bigger and better appliances. It makes sense, then, that we've loosened our rules about counters, formerly a uniform expanse of a single material.

Deciding which material should grace each area comes down to two basic considerations: Is the surface designated for work (cooking and cleaning) or for play (entertain-

[OPPOSITE] KITCHENS USED TO BE A SINGLE UNIVERSAL SURFACE. NOW WE MIX AND MATCH. FREEDOM OF CHOICE CREATES OTHER CONCERNS. WHEN MIXING SURFACES, CHOOSE WHAT YOU LIKE TEMPERED BY WHAT WORKS BEST WHERE.

No matter the surface—even butcher block or granite—it's smart to use a cutting board when slicing and dicing. While you can peel fruit or butter a bagel directly on a counter's surface, whenever you use a knife, you risk a nick.

ing and socializing)? Certain materials are better suited to certain jobs. You might, for example, use marble, a cool-to-the-touch surface ideal for rolling out pastry, in a baking zone, and stainless steel, a heat-resistant metal, surrounding the stove. Or you might specify teak on an island used largely for socializing and zinc for a bar area used primarily to stir up cocktails. The counter on either side of the sink is the most heavily used in the kitchen. Between splashing water, steel wool scrubbies, and food scraps, the sink area demands the most durable and water-resistant materials available, whether granite, solid synthetic, or stainless steel.

You'll also want to factor in the color, cost, and character of a surface. A stone countertop, for instance, is colder than anything around it. While marble won't cool your entire kitchen on a hot, muggy morning, it sure will chill any ready-to-serve dinner plates you set down on it—faster than you might imagine. In my kitchen, I never put my morning tea directly on our limestone countertop. A wood island is warmer, cozier, and perhaps more welcoming, if that is where you are going to take all of your kitchen meals. If there's no room for a breakfast table, you might consider a teak, maple, or walnut center island. Once you've weighed the pros and cons of each type and gotten some feedback from fellow renovators as well as designers, architects, and family members, the best choice or choices for your project will rise to the surface.

FORMICA (PICTURED IN THE CABINETS IN THE REAR) CAN ALSO BE CHIC, WHEN DRESSED UP WITH STYLISH HARDWARE.

The Laminates

The most affordable choice also happens to be the most often chosen. Laminates—man-made thin plastics glued over a wood base—account for two-thirds of all countertop choices (a statistic surprising to me!). That's because, simply put, they look pretty good for the price. Laminates come in a huge range of colors and patterns. My advice: Pick a laminate that looks like a laminate, not one that pretends to be a stone, wood, or (can you believe it?) leather. Let it be what it is. Because the design is actually printed onto the laminate surface, attempts to mimic nature tend to come off as cartoonish. Either go with a basic solid or use some of the wonderful and forgiving textural prints that are just that—such as Canvas, Sisal, and Glaze—with no delusions of grandeur.

On a purely pragmatic level, laminates are easy to maintain. Cleaning is as simple as using a mild detergent and a damp sponge. And they're durable . . . to a degree. Chipping and scratching can mar the surface of most laminates, making a cutting board a must. At the high end of the laminate family is a material called Colorcore that won't show the chips as much; it's solid plastic all the way through rather than a laminate veneer layered over plywood. Knife nicks or scratches expose more of the same laminate surface instead of

FIELD NOTE

In his bachelor pad, with its galley-style kitchen that opened to the living room, Matt Kearns chose a classic green-gray granite, called Verde Maritaka, for all of the counter surfaces—except for one: an elevated shelf (at a 42-inch bar height) that was added over the counter dividing the living room and cooking area. This second tier, elevated 6 inches above the peninsula and mounted on discreet stainless-steel dowels, was made of glass, not granite. The glass is not only lighter in weight than stone but also lighter in look. And while it does not provide a solid screen of privacy, it does create a visual interruption between the living and cooking spaces, lifting the counter to new heights. As it turns out, the ledge has also become a great ad-hoc buffet and bar, thus serving the apartment in more than one way.

the plywood. But even this plastic is not perfect. Like all laminates, Colorcore can become unglued at the edges when water gets underneath, and once delaminated, the damage is irreparable (wipe up standing water immediately to guard against this). Still, with proper care, a laminate countertop can last ten or more years.

The Premier Plastics

A cut far, far above laminates is the category of plastics known as solid surfaces. Made of polyester or acrylic resin with mineral fillers, the composites (DuPont Corian, Avonite, and Swanstone are among the better known) have the durability and longevity of stone—and a similar price tag. The look, however, is clearly and proudly something else.

These high-end synthetics actually have some advantages over stone, as well as over the lower-priced laminates. For one thing, they're seamless. No matter how long or complicated the run of countertop, and no matter what shape you want to cut (straight, curved, or serpentine), you won't have to deal with hiding seams or joints. The uninterrupted expanse of smoothness is sleek and modern-looking, and in white or ivory, such a solid surface can embody the so-called laboratory look and create a clean, unobtrusive, neutral backdrop in a kitchen. These premiere plastics also come in a sizable range of colors and textures, so you have the option of making a stronger visual statement. I like the speckled or stippled ones best; in addition to being impervious, they hide crumbs and stray salt and sugar granules, so at least I *think* the counter is clean. Solid surfaces, for the most part, don't try to pass themselves off as marble or granite or some other stone found in nature. Rather, they're honestly appealing, not pretentious, and have a cachet all their own. Unlike laminates, which are surface-printed, solid surfaces are patterned through and through. What's more, the speckled patterns—what I think of as cake batter—encompass a mix of hues, offering a great way to bridge a mix of colors and design elements in a kitchen.

Solid surfaces are also nearly indestructible. Because they're nonporous, they're impervious to most stains, although not completely heat resistant. And because they're one material through and through, you can sand or buff out the occasional small blemish with a little steel wool. They also have a long lifespan; in fact, many come with a twenty-year warranty.

[ABOVE] CREAMY WHITE CORIAN CREATES A CLEAN LABORATORY LOOK AND WORK SURFACE AND WARMS RIGHT UP WHEN PARTNERED WITH HONED BLACK GRANITE.

FIELD NOTE

Alissa Hackmann had decided early in the renovation process that she wanted a cream-colored stone with coffee-colored markings, called Leche de Luna, for her new kitchen counters. The soft markings and the hue of Leche, a quartzite new to the stone yard, perfectly wrapped up the decorative elements of the space—hardwood floors, warm white-glazed cabinets, a stainless-steel fridge, and a taupe Viking range. She visited the marble yard and placed two slabs on hold about two months before she needed them; most yards won't warehouse a stone any earlier than that, and besides, all those months in storage just invite breakage.

And so, feeling confident, she met with the fabricator a month before installation for final approval. Then, whoops. She was stunned to see that the slabs she had chosen had stronger-than-anticipated diagonal lines running through them and a blindingly white rivulet, perpendicular to the diagonal lines, that she couldn't ignore. How could she have missed those flaws?

There was no bait-and-switch involved; these were, in fact, the slabs she had chosen. The truth is that it's often hard, in a dimly lit marble yard, to see every fleck and flaw. What's more, stone fabricators cringe at the notion of characterizing these markings as flaws at all. Each fissure or pop of crystal is simply sediment, a marking unique to that particular slab of stone, and by no means a "flaw."

Fortunately, a clever fabricator, Jim Spader of Millennium Stone, was able to manipulate the stone's cuts into different locations and seam the slabs in such a way that he buried the less desirable markings in a corner where the toaster and coffeemaker would sit. And he was able to cut the slab with the white rivulet on either side of the mark and use the flanking pieces for the smaller countertops by the kitchen's range. The slender sliver containing the rivulet was relegated to the fabricator's floor, where such pieces are labeled *droppings*. Ultimately, Alissa was able to adopt this mantra: Embrace the flaws.

The Composites

Silestone, Cesarstone, Zodiaq—these are some of the exotic-sounding names in an exploding category of hybrid countertops labeled *engineered stones*. They're made almost entirely of quartz (93 percent), a real stone, with just a little polymer and pigment (7 percent) added to the mix—think of jeans with a bit of Lycra. This new and rapidly growing breed of countertop runs the gamut, stylewise, from a freckled "granite" to a bright apple-green "stone," and it has the distinctive advantage of being less expensive than stone.

The hybrids have many of the virtues and few of the short-comings of true stone countertops. These composites come as a single, uniform slab, without natural imperfections, making them stronger than marble or granite (which have natural faults and fissures) and less likely to chip and crack—especially important during installation. Because they're nonporous (which means no sealant is required), composites are proof against stains, scratches, and water—even more so than stone. Some of them, like Silestone, are even germ-resistant (an antimicrobial chemical is added to the polymer). What's next?!

Great as hybrids are, they come with a caveat: Too much perfection is not always a good thing. Composites lack the beauty and rhythm of natural stone's veins and splotches—and sometimes that serendipitous, uneven marking is just what's needed for character. Unfortunately, composites ultimately look like what they are—man-made. You also run a slight risk, as you do with any manufactured material, that the manufacturer will drop your pattern or color, leaving you in the lurch if you want to add more of the same in the future—to an island or a backsplash for instance. There's debate, too, about the stone's hand; some homeowners object to what they call a resin feel, while others view engineered stone as neither plastic-like or stone-like but agreeably otherworldly.

The Natural Stones

Americans have finally discovered what Europeans and South Americans have known for centuries: Nothing looks as beautiful as natural stone countertops. Walk through a stone yard and you'll find slabs from Italy and France alongside those from more unexpected sources, such as

[LEFT] WHEN A STONE SURFACE EXTENDS IN SEVERAL DIFFERENT DIRECTIONS BE SURE THAT THE PATTERN INHERENT IN THE STONE IS PLEASING TO YOUR EYE, ANY WHICH WAY IT GOES.

Turkey, Iran, and Brazil. No matter the provenance of the stones, the beauty and variation is awe-inspiring. How can the earth yield such incredible outpourings?

Transported into a kitchen, stone adds a rare richness—and the rarer the stone, the higher the cost. But while expensive, stone can be viewed as a smart investment; it comes out on top (of other countertop surfaces) in terms of keeping its value should you ever decide to sell. A major part of its appeal, both to you and to prospective buyers down the road, is its uniqueness.

Consider carefully how prominent or quiet you want the pattern to be. If you're going to be laying stone around all of the perimeter counters in the kitchen, you probably want to avoid markings that are too directional (especially if your counters do a U-turn, meaning the stone runs north, south, east, and west) or too pronounced, with a proliferation of lava flows and rivulets or chips and flakes. The overall effect will simply have too much movement—chaos-inducing! On the other hand, a stone with strong and idiosyncratic markings might be just the statement that's needed for an island. Visualize how the stone will work in concert with the rest of the space. A heavily veined marble may be stunning in isolation but come off as too loud in the company of highly wrought cabinets or a checkerboard floor.

If you choose to use more than one type of stone countertop—and a mix can be done to great effect, provided at least one of the stones has subdued markings—factor in your budget that you'll run up extra costs, as each stone will require a separate installation and there will likely be more droppings—that is, wasted pieces. Then there's the whole resale issue: Some Realtors contend that an overly eclectic kitchen can turn off a potential buyer.

When selecting slabs, be sure to see the prospective pieces in all their glory and imperfection at the stone supplier. I discovered this the hard way early in my career. I chose a rich green marble for an island in a prewar Manhattan building—based on a lovely 4-inch sample. The day the counter was installed, I received a panicked phone call from the customer. Was there supposed to be a freckle the size of, well, Manhattan in the middle of the island? Needless to say, I replaced the island counter and learned my lesson.

Also inquire about the size of the slab; most average 6 to 8 feet. On a long run of counters, you will most likely need to join two slabs, which creates a visible seam. Position seams as far from the sink as possible; despite the skill of the fabricator, a seam near the sink is doused with water constantly. After a year or two, it's not unusual to find water has seeped into the seam and thence the subsurface of the stone, setting the stage for future cracks.

If you are ordering slabs of the same stone at two different times, make sure the slabs marry well—that they have compatible markings. Don't assume that because you order two pieces of the same stone they will necessarily look the same. One may have a dusting of freckles, the other conspicuous blotches. Even when you order your slabs all at once, there may be some disparities. Different stones have different patterns of disparity. Granite, for instance, may have nearly identical markings throughout but will get progressively darker the deeper in the quarry it was discovered. With marble, the colors will likely be close in hue, but the location of the veins may shift—a little or a lot. You need to order two slices

TRADE TIP

Be open minded about buying stones quarried from little-known locales. In fact, you may have no choice! When I last asked to see Ivory Gold, the warm gold and cream stone veined and flecked with charcoal that I have often requested at the local stone supplier, I was told it "*was* a beautiful stone." Past tense. The Indian quarry from which it was excavated is now closed. End of stone and end of story.

Fortunately, there are many, many new quarries being opened all the time—chips off the new block, as it were—including granite quarries in Brazil and marble and onyx quarries in the Middle East. In this case, I was able to find the last few slabs of Ivory Gold at a marble yard in North Carolina.

TRADE TIP

Stone is about 15 degrees colder to the touch than anything around it. A stone counter is a ready-made pastry board, ideal for rolling out piecrust or kneading bread. But a boon for the baker is bane for people who are always cold. If you don't bake, think twice about all stone everywhere. A wood countertop for chopping is warmer.

[TOP] EVERY SLAB OF STONE IS UNIQUE, WITH ITS OWN DISTINCTIVE MARKINGS. TAKE A PHOTO OF YOUR SELECTION AT THE MARBLE YARD TO AVOID CONFUSION OR SWITCHES.

[ABOVE] WITH A DUPONT EDGE AND A GRACEFUL FRENCH CURVE-SCRIBED BACKSPLASH A GENERIC STONE BECOMES A STANDOUT.

cut from the same slab, and set eyes on both, to be sure they will be good partners.

As for durability, here's a truth no one likes to admit: All stone counters stain to some degree. How much, exactly, is a matter of three factors: hardness (the harder the stone, the more resistance to scratches), porosity (how open the pores are), and, somewhat surprisingly, pattern. Heavily marked stones have a built-in concealer factor in their favor. One person's blot is another person's mark of character. I say embrace the flaws and blemishes. Perfection comes at a very high price.

Marble

Homeowners are often dissuaded from using marble by marble yards, fabricators, and kitchen stores alike—it's too porous, you'll hear, or too stain-prone. While it's true that marble is apt to stain or etch (it's particularly vulnerable to wine, lemon, and orange juice), it's also true that hundred-year-old marble counters that have aged beautifully fill French bakeries; it's hard to know where a vein ends and a stain begins. In fact, marble, along with limestone, now accounts for about thirty percent of all stone counter sales. The reason is relatively clear-cut: If you have your heart set on the mellowness of marble, with its fluid, graceful markings, nothing else will compare. Of the many varieties, Carerra (the classic baker's marble), Statutory White (pristine white with gray markings), and Verde (soft green) are timeless classics—and, as an interesting side note, these particular marbles have actually gotten a bit less expensive over the years as their popularity has increased.

Granite

Granite loyalists love the stone's swirls and whorls, and its palette, which ranges from earthy browns to solid black. Available in a huge number of nuanced colors and patterns, granite is being quarried more than ever before, and from a broader range of countries, including Brazil, where new quarries open almost weekly. The upshot is that granite prices have actually fallen over the last few years.

There's no doubt that granite is durable; it's nearly impossible to scratch or etch, it's heatproof and waterproof, and it does not deteriorate with age. But it's not for those who value subtlety. The overall speckles can come off as busy, not to mention boring, and the most expensive slabs often have a sparkly crystalline quality that makes them the center of attention in a flashy sort of way.

To my eye, this is a stone that looks best in medium to light hues (darker colors can appear murky and turbid) and honed, which is to say stripped of its polish. Also, the stone's hardness cuts two ways: Even as it adds to the stone's toughness, it rules out elaborate edge detailing.

FIELD NOTE

The owners of a shingle-style summer cottage on the coast of Maine insisted on installing historically appropriate soapstone counters when renovating their 1887 kitchen. While the visual effect was terrific, the maintenance became a family battle. No one wanted the chore of applying a monthly dose of mineral oil—and no one wanted to touch the counters the morning after, when the tacky residue required follow-up elbow grease and a roll of paper towels to work in.

Fast-forward a few years to when the family's primary urban home kitchen needed an upgrade. This time, they decided to eschew real soapstone and order black granite counters, stripped of their shine, for a soapstone-like effect without the drudgery of monthly oiling. And guess what? The granite just never looked right. It wasn't organic; it never turned lighter with wear or mellowed with age. In retrospect, the family wished they'd chosen soapstone, elbow grease and all.

Limestone Limestone is generally light-colored (in the ivory/yellow family) and has few markings, giving it a minimalist appeal. Clean and sleek, limestone has a calming effect, especially welcome when there's a lot going on visually in a kitchen. While stone suppliers complain that limestone is fragile and stain-prone, my experience says otherwise. It's been fifteen years and counting since we installed limestone on our kitchen island, complete with a zillion-BTU professional range, and we have but one small ding and not a single stain (stains in the making are simply buffed out with a little kitchen scrubbie or a bit of steel wool).

Soapstone Understated soapstone manages to look both vintage and modern at the same time. Sometimes called architectural soapstone (to distinguish it from artistic soapstone, a softer variety), this blue-gray, lightly flecked stone is still quarried in New England. The stone has a high talc content, which lends it a matte, velvety finish. Long used in school science labs, it's impervious to whatever chemical mishaps students (or cooks) dream up—even red wine and lemon, the usual enemies of stone counters. Slabs typically run no longer than 4 to 6 feet, so plan placement—and seams—carefully. On the topic of care: Soapstone needs TLC. The stone requires monthly oiling with a spritz of mineral or olive oil to keep it looking rich.

Quartzite Just now emerging as a suitable choice for kitchen counters, quartzite is the hardest stone, harder than granite, even. It is similarly heat- and water-resistant, and its colors are generally paler than granites, with soft and fluid markings. The rub: Quartzite is quite porous. It must be sealed upon installation and resealed every six months or so to stay looking immaculate.

Slate It's a cheaper alternative to granite and marble, a bit harder than soapstone and also less expensive, but slate comes with a slew of issues. Many slates are just plain too porous for the kitchen. Slate is particularly prone to oil absorption and discoloration, and its natural clefts make for an uneven work surface. What's more, it tends to come in small slabs, leading to the need for more seams. Still, some homeowners swear by slate—which comes in shades of brown, gray, and green—for seldom-used counters, choosing to embrace the inevitable flaws as personality. A few newer slates are less porous and more suitable. Ask for a slate with a high silica content, which makes it sturdier and less likely to flake.

Honed stone is like buffed nails. The overall effect is matte, and the lustrous finish is easy to maintain. There are two levels of honing. With high-honed stone, my preference, the slab is polished with less pressure and grit to yield a satin sheen. With normal or low honing, the stone is sanded with very fine grit and can come off as flat-looking and pasty. In either case, you will probably want to color-enhance your stone prior to honing to bring out the beauty of the natural color. Because honing dulls the stone—sometimes to such a degree that it looks lifeless—a relatively inexpensive process called color enhancing, done on site at the marble yard, uses an impregnating sealer to add color to the stone without adding shine.

TRADE TIP

Stones are sold in a unique and anachronistic way. The slab of stone you select at a marble yard is sold to a fabricator—*not* to the builder or contractor or even to you. The fabricator is responsible for making the template to fit your counters, for cutting the stone, and for the installing it as well.

[ABOVE] IN MY BOOK, THE SUBTLE SHEEN OF A HONED LIMESTONE, OR ANY STONE FOR THAT MATTER, FAR OUTLASTS THE GLITZY SHINE OF ITS POLISHED SISTER.

THE SHINE FACTOR

With either marble or granite, you have a choice of how you want the slab finished: polished or honed. An enormous polishing machine, complete with more than twenty heads running over the slab, applies polishing powders to the stone to achieve a mirror-like polish. Each application uses a progressively finer grit. Like a manicure, a high-gloss finish is difficult to maintain. It wears off in areas of high use—around the sink, where cleansers abrade, and near the stove, where you put down pots and stack plates. Be aware that a polished surface is highly reflective; light can bounce off the countertops into your eyes, not to mention off metal appliances like toasters or microwaves, which creates double images on the countertop itself. So why do people still request polish? It adds a layer of protection—the higher the polish, the more impervious the surface. If you're neurotically careful about maintenance, or if you've chosen a porous stone such as quartzite, you may prefer a polished surface because it will simply look more pristine.

The Care and Feeding of Stone

When it comes to stone, an ounce of prevention, by way of protective sealers, is all important. Simply put, sealers repel spills. That doesn't mean you can leave spills sitting endlessly atop your counter. The sealer buys you time to wipe up before the offending substance soaks in.

Stone's biggest enemies are orange juice, vinegar, red wine, soy sauce, tomatoes, mustard, and coffee. These acidic foods can etch into the counter's surface, eating away at the polished surface or etching the honed stone and leaving blobs and marks. Fortunately, such marks are not indelible, even if left overnight. That was the case when my husband made homemade spaghetti sauce one evening. I returned home late to a delicious pasta and woke the next morning to red splatters on our limestone countertop. Luckily, we'd recently resealed the counter, and the spots came up with a plastic scrubbie and elbow grease.

So what's the story with sealers? First of all, they can go by any number of names, including revitalizers, polishers, and enhancers. No matter the moniker, the job is the same: to prevent spills from infiltrating the surface and keep a counter's shine or sheen up to snuff. While there are many good sealers and sealants (the terms are used interchangeably) on the market—Porous Plus 511 and Bullet Proof from Stone Tech, for example—you should make sure the product is made especially for stone. Steer clear of harsh household cleansers. Ask yourself if you'd use something like that on your car—chances are, probably not. Some sealers do double duty by both protecting the stone and enhancing its natural color. Ask the stone installer—who is the first to seal the stone in situ—what has been used, and then order an extra can to keep on hand.

Once a stone is sealed, you likely won't have to do it again for quite some time. Granites might need resealing once or twice a year; limestones and marbles warrant a quarterly application. How to know when it's time? There are two quickie tests. Splash a few water drops on the counter; if the water beads, you're still under seal; if not, it's time to reapply. Alternatively, in a small, inconspicuous corner, spritz a little mineral oil on the counter; if the oil stays on the surface, you're fine; if it soaks in, it's time to reseal.

When the time does come, applying sealer is pretty simple. First, thoroughly clean the stone with a spray cleaner (Windex, a more gentle cleanser, or the like). Then just pour the sealer (it is clear, like water) on a clean white cloth and apply to the counter in small sections with a circular motion. Let the sealer sit for several minutes and then wipe the counter dry with a new clean cloth, buffing as you go and making sure to remove excess product to prevent streaking.

The Outsiders

Outdoor materials most typically used underfoot are making their way inside and up onto the counter. Terrazzo, once exclusively a patio stone, is one such candidate for floors and countertops alike. A mix of granite and marble chips, recycled glass, and shells set in cement and then polished to a smooth surface, terrazzo can offer an unusual, decorative twist to a kitchen. The color possibilities are virtually unlimited, depending on which stones and chips are used, making originality one of terrazzo's strongest selling points. Additionally, terrazzo is waterproof and quite durable, though a tad less so than solid stone. It also happens to be expensive and somewhat tricky to install.

Concrete, while not as pretty (or eco-friendly) as terrazzo, has an earthy kind of chic. But unless it's extremely well buffed, it's rough to the touch, dull-looking (even when dyed), and heavy (you need to overbuild base cabinets to support it). Also, concrete has to be sealed and resealed regularly—monthly even—as it can stain. Last, it cracks like the San Andreas fault.

Volcanic stones (yes, as in lava) are refined-looking, impervious to stains, and just as expensive as concrete. An Italian variety known as Basaltina is flecked with specks of ash and fissures and is particularly beautiful. The slab sizes tend to be small, but the palette is understated and subtle, in soft browns and grays.

[BELOW] PATTERN CAN OVERPOWER. USE STRONG PATTERN IN SMALL DOSES. WHEN MIXING, A SCALE CHANGE IS CRITICAL OR THE PATTERNS WILL START TO SWARM.

The Tiles

Tiles can add a pop of color, a touch of shine, and, depending on the type, a sense of hand-crafted quality. Most homeowners and builders choose ceramic for a counter, as these tiles are resistant to heat, stains, and water. Porcelains are another wise choice. They offer consistent quality and are designed to resemble everything from soapstone to slate to lava. Glass tiles, while translucently beautiful, are too fragile for a work surface, and terra-cotta, a rustic tile normally relegated to floors, tends to be too uneven for a counter.

Regardless of the type of tile you choose, it will require grout—which, in turn, requires extra maintenance, as crumbs and liquids tend to collect in the creases. What's more, the grout is apt to darken over time. To minimize this effect, install a tile countertop with tight joints and use a darker-colored grout to start with.

CUTTING EDGES

The same logic applies to edge details as to counter surfaces themselves: You'll determine the edge that suits your stone based on the rest of your kitchen surroundings. A clean, simple edge works well on the perimeter countertops, which tend to be flanked by cabinets, crowded with coffeemakers and dish drainers, and full of distractions. A fancy edge may get lost in the shuffle. In the case of an island, however, which is essentially a stand-alone, four-sided piece of furniture, a graceful, decorative edge, like the serpentine ogee, can be beautiful. No matter the profile, edge detailings can be fashioned out of any stone—or any solid surface, for that matter—in widths from ¾ inch to 2 inches.

Here, a quick education in styles of edges:

- **EASED.** A 90-degree edge with the sharp corners softened just a bit.

- **BEVEL.** A 45-degree angle from top to side. Bevel can be from ⅛ inch to ¾ inch.

- **PENCIL.** Rounded like the used tip of a Number 2 pencil.

- **DEMI-BULL** or **HALF BULLNOSE.** A rounded pencil edge with a greater radius.

- **DUPONT.** A demi-bull with an extra step at the top to create a secondary level.

- **FULL-BULL.** A fully rounded edge, more popular on furniture than countertops.

- **OGEE.** A cascading edge with a complex curvature—concave, convex, concave.

- **ROMAN OGEE.** An ogee with an extra flourish.

The Woods

Wood is an oldie and, in the right situation, a goodie. It has a natural warmth that makes an appealing countertop. It won't blunt knives or break your dishes. What's more, most stains and scorch marks can be sanded out on the spot.

Of all the many species of wood available, the densest ones, like maple and teak, are the most counter-intelligent. Long used on boats, teak is the hardest wood of all. As a countertop, it's usually lacquered on both sides for shine and protection. Be aware that sitting liquids can eventually dissolve the lacquer and that knives can scratch its surface.

Other species qualify as counter material as well—some more so than others. Butcher block is made of small planks of solid maple glued together; the strongest and densest type is known as end grain. Cherry has a wavy, watery grain more appropriate on the vertical plane or in a library. The grain of oak has too much movement and noise for a countertop. Mahogany is elegant but a bit dressy. Pine is generally considered too soft, unless you find the accumulated scuff marks and dings part of the charm.

In general, oiled woods are more heat-resistant than lacquered woods, though they still may warp or crack in big swings of humidity (as in an overheated or excessively air-conditioned space). A monthly coating of mineral oil keeps the wood from growing brittle.

Any way you slice it, a wood countertop is a commitment. It demands sealing and resealing over the years as your stain and sealer wear away. And because wood is an open-grained surface, it requires occasional scrubbing with antibacterial soap after exposure to certain foods, like raw chicken, or to get rid of lingering odors, such as onion or garlic. From an aesthetic standpoint, don't go overboard on wood. As much as I like the look and feel of wood, I like it best in small amounts. A teak island, for example, is the perfect touch of warmth in a sea of gleaming white.

[ABOVE] A BEST-OF-BOTH-WORLDS APPROACH TO COUNTERS: RICH OAK ADDS WARMTH TO AN ISLAND WHILE STONE FLANKS THE REAL WORK-HORSES OF THE KITCHEN—THE SINK AND THE STOVE.

[OPPOSITE] THE PRICE OF A TEAK COUNTER DEPENDS UPON THE WIDTH OF THE PLANKS (TOO WIDE AND THEY MIGHT WARP OR MOVE) AND THE THICKNESS OF THE WOOD. INSTEAD OF ORDERING A COUNTER THAT'S 2 INCHES THICK, CONSIDER GOING WITH A 1-INCH DIMENSION AND ADDING A TRIM PIECE OF ANOTHER INCH.

COUNTER MEASURES

The dimensions of a counter affect both price and look. Here are rules of thumb:

- **THE THICKNESS.** Counters range from ¾ inch (the old standard) all the way up to 2 inches (a modern, more European look). Many suppliers suggest a middle ground: 1¼ inches. While that looks fine to my eye, I also favor the thinner ¾-inch counters, which have the advantage of being considerably less expensive.

- **THE OVERHANG.** An overhang of ¾ inch is standard. Any less, and you bump up against the underlying cabinet handles and hardware as you lean in to work. Any more, and you throw the cabinets into shadow.

When it comes to an island, where seating is involved, you want enough counter space to comfortably tuck your legs (and stools) under. The optimum overhang is 13 inches, though anything over 10 inches will work (I've even specified 8 inches where space was tight—far better than nothing). With an overhang of up to 13 inches, no additional support is needed, given a countertop that is either ¾ inch or 1¼ inches thick. If the stone is fragile, however, a fabricator may suggest inserting steel rods in the underside of the stone for stability. Remember, stone is exceptionally heavy, and a large cantilevered surface invites toppling. For overhangs greater than 13 inches, be sure to have your carpenter or cabinetmaker add brackets for support.

The Metals

Stainless steel, that silvery, industrial metal, would make for a nearly perfect countertop if durability were the only consideration. Noncorrosive and heatproof, stainless is easy to clean and extremely hygienic. Other than a seamless synthetic, stainless is the only material that allows for a one-piece surface and sink.

Stainless does, however, show wear and tear—namely, scratches and fingerprints. Even though fingerprints and smudges come off easily, you'll find yourself cleaning them more frequently with stainless. What's more, certain liquids can dull the finish, creating matte areas. The shinier the finish, the more visible the flaws; a brushed finish is the most forgiving. Brushed or not, stainless steel is hard to live with—especially in large amounts. I once visited a Manhattan kitchen done entirely in stainless steel, and I found it exceptionally cold and clattery. I couldn't imagine living there day in and day out. If nothing but stainless will suffice for you, however, you can at least cut down on the noise factor by gluing insulation board to the undersides of countertops. And make sure to go for a higher grade and lower gauge. The lower the gauge (that is, the higher the chromium and nickel content), the longer-lasting the surface. Some stainless counters last up to fifteen years.

When used judiciously, stainless steel is undeniably striking. I love my stainless-steel double sink with attached drainboard. But I like it because it's balanced with other surfaces, like wood and stone. Too much metal, as that Manhattan kitchen proved, can look antiseptic—the dreaded cafeteria kitchen comes to mind.

A few other metals worth their mettle include copper and zinc. Both have romantic associations—think of bars in Paris bistros. Both metals, however, are susceptible to scratches and dents, a bit more so than stainless steel. Copper requires frequent heavy-duty polishing to maintain its shine. Pewter counters, another French import, can add an unusual and handsome touch in a butler's pantry or bar area, but not near a stove, as pewter has a low melting point. These metals have what designers call, euphemistically, living finishes. Translated loosely, that means that they won't continue looking like they did on delivery, no matter how lovingly you treat them. While these metals require high-maintenance, in small doses their distinctiveness may be worth the extra effort.

The Backsplash

The backsplash is where splashes leave their mark—on the wall behind the stove, the sink, or under the upper cabinets. Made from tile or stone in a range of colors from creamy white to cobalt blue, or even enameled wood, the backsplash is designed to protect those vulnerable areas with a surface that resists both water and stains.

Interestingly, while the kitchen itself has grown larger over the last decade—outfitted with supersized appliances, generous windows, and tall cabinets that come all the way down to meet the counter—the backsplash is one element that's gotten smaller. It is still a place to make a style statement, however, whether you choose to run it under all the upper cabinetry for visual continuity or highlight just one or two areas and make them pop.

While the physical size of the backsplash may be decreasing, the material choices are greater than ever. You could opt for a stone one to match your countertop—a honeyed limestone backsplash

TRADE TIP

Your backsplash must have a waterproof joint where it meets the countertop to keep moisture from getting under the counter and warping the plywood subcounter (in the case of laminates) or the back of the base cabinet (in the case of stones). Although counter or tile installers worth their salt should know this, it doesn't hurt to remind them.

[OPPOSITE] A STANDARD 4-INCH BACKSPLASH MEANS YOU HAVE TO COME UP WITH YET ANOTHER SURFACE FOR THE SPACE BETWEEN SPLASH AND UPPER CABINETS, THAT IS. WALLPAPER, MORE WASHABLE THAN PAINT, IS A SMART CHOICE.

TRADE TIP

It's a long reach to clean a backsplash. Think twice about a textured or extruded tile with a raised design in relief. Grease has a way of settling in the grooves and recesses, becoming a prime tacky attraction for flour, dust, and spices. A smoother surface is easier to wipe down. And go for a darkish grout, in tight lines, to help conceal dirt or grime that may settle back there.

that wraps up the wall, for instance. Or you could choose to put up a wainscot splash, painted in glossy enamel to repel water. And, of course, a tile backsplash is still a great way to go, and usually my preference, especially given the many decorative choices. Suffice it to say that we've moved well beyond the once ubiquitous tiles of sweet botanicals or lyrical, pastoral scenes of the Loire Valley. You might have your backsplash clad in subway tiles for a chic, minimalist look or in faceted glass mosaic tiles that lend a luminescent quality to the kitchen's décor.

Tiles

Going to a tile store is a bit like walking into a candy store; the zillions of choices are tantalizing and sometimes overwhelming. How to pick from this shade of white or that hue of blue? They are all so appealing.

No one will be walking on your backsplash tiles—fine news, from a practical standpoint. Unlike a floor, which has to hold up to foot traffic and provide a no-skid surface, the backsplash is a vertical plane; all you have to worry about is pleasing your eye. In fact, the backsplash is the one place in the kitchen—maybe in the entire house—where you can indulge just about any whim or taste, from riotous color to a crackled glaze. While liquids and spills might spash on your spash, that's a far rarer occurrence than on countertops.

So how, then, to narrow the choices from the aisles of tiles? The first decision you might make, one that will affect both look and price, is whether you're going to go with handmade or machine-made tiles. The handmade type has its appeal, if you like the authenticity of subtle irregularities, but it costs considerably more than the uniform, more perfect look of machine-made tiles.

In either category, you'll have a kaleidoscope of hues from which to choose. My only word of advice here: subtlety. While you may be drawn to bright colors or elaborate patterns, it's often better to err on the side of the understated. A loud backsplash runs the risk of competing with, rather than complementing, the cabinets and counters, not to mention adding visual jumble to an area already busy with the coffeemaker, toaster, oils, vinegars, paper towels, and other countertop clutter.

TRADE TIP

It's a fair bet that some tiles will have to be trimmed to fit in the space for your backsplash. The question—and the artistry—lies in where those cuts occur. The goal is to keep the center of the backsplash whole, pristine, and uncut. That's where your eye goes. Once the center tiles are aligned, then the outermost pieces can be trimmed as needed. Aim to keep both the top and bottom tiles of similar sizes. Ask the installer to cut them both by 1 inch, for instance, rather than lopping 2 inches off one or the other. The more symmetrical the cuts, the more polished the overall look.

[ABOVE] MESH-MOUNTED GLASS TILES SIZZLE ON A BACKSPLASH, REFLECTING LIGHT AND ILLUMINATING THE DARK RECESSES.

FIELD NOTE

Judy Zern of Westchester County was surprised when her natural beige grout turned her green opalescent glass backsplash tile darker and decidedly less sea green. She had picked the beige because she figured it would have been hard to keep a white grout clean in a kitchen. What she discovered, to her initial dismay, was that the tan shade of the grout muted the delicate green tiles with a slight brownish cast. However, in the end, the beige grout turned out to be the right choice. When the butcher-block counters were installed and the oak floor laid, stained, and sealed, the natural beige grout looked right at home.

Color isn't the only choice you'll have to make. You'll also need to decide on the size of the tile. The average backsplash area is about 16 inches tall. Obviously, the larger the tiles, the fewer of them you'll need to cover a given surface area. Fewer tiles means less grout—an advantage, certainly pragmatically, as grout collects dirt and grease. Fewer tiles also means a cleaner overall look, since fewer lines of grout will interrupt the expanse of tile. But a small tile has its charm. In fact, the tiniest glass mosaic tiles—no more than 1 or 2 inches each—can create a field of faceted glistening color—or, when laid in a particular pattern, depict a striking design. And even though mosaics are small, they typically come on a mesh backing of a foot square or more, which makes them quite easy to install. But back to the grout issue: To make cleaning all those little filler lines easier, ask the installer to use a smooth grout rather than the sand-textured variety, which tends to attract dirt and crumbs.

Add a fresh look to your backsplash by having tiles installed in unique or counterintuitive ways. Tiles can be laid in a basketweave pattern or a herringbone, straight and narrow or interrupted with a decorative trim piece either of the same tile or something completely unexpected. Add a racing stripe in a sharp new color, or create a checkerboard by alternating colors every second or third tile. The same basic square-shaped tile feels new when turned on its point, forming a harlequin, or when applied to the wall with its joints staggered brick style rather than lining up in a grid. The display boards in a showroom offer much inspiration, but it's worth taking home as many samples as possible and playing with designs and patterns in situ. Stack the tiles vertically, ideally atop your counter surface of choice. Stagger, rotate, interrupt, and build your kitchen scenario. Only that way will you be able to really see what suits your space.

Stone

As stone countertops have flourished, so have stone backsplashes—and for good reason. Stone, whether marble, honed granite, or soapstone, is hardworking and handsome. Granted, stone of any type is expensive, but when you limit it to the relatively small area of a backsplash, you

[LEFT] A FULL-HEIGHT STONE BACKSPLASH IS THE WAY TO GO IF YOUR BUDGET ALLOWS: NO GROUT, NO GROOVES, AND NO SEAM MAKE FOR A CLEAN AND EASY SWEEP WHEN THE COUNTER NEEDS A SWIPE.

ZEROING IN ON THE RANGE

The spot directly behind the range is a natural focal point in the kitchen, and one you can play up or play down. One approach is to take a cue from the hood itself. With a stainless-steel hood, for instance, you might want to use the backsplash space to reinforce an industrial restaurant look by running a full-height sheet of steel from the range to the vent. If your range hood is more decorative—fashioned like a wooden mantel or a plaster hearth—you can underscore the country look with tiles in a crackled finish. Decorative and ornamental medallions depicting flower- and fruit-filled baskets, once the must-have feature of an upscale kitchen backsplash, have lost their cachet. A simpler take, framing out a square of contrasting or directionally different tiles with a clean linear tile strip, says "medallion" without the emblematic (and easy to date) centerpiece.

[ABOVE] THE RAP ON STAINLESS STEEL IS THAT IT SHOWS ITS AGE. NOT ALWAYS: THIS COUNTER HAS BEEN IN PLACE FOR MORE THAN SIXTY YEARS AND STILL LOOKS GREAT.

limit the cost as well. If you're committed to the concept, make sure you execute the idea well. Use the same type of slab for counter and backsplash for a truly seamless look. Using two different kinds of stones can come off looking like too much—too much pattern, too much movement in the whorls and swirls. Tumbled marble, the "it" stone for many a renovator, has a worn and rutted look. But I'd think twice about using tumbled marble for a backsplash; it has too much texture and patina to be paired with anything other than a smooth, clean surface like Corian.

Metals

Metal, whether the typical stainless or the more exotic copper or zinc, makes a perfectly suitable backsplash surface. It's water-resistant, a breeze to wipe clean (no grout lines to worry about), and its slightly reflective surface brings a bit of shine and life to an area often in the shadow—literally— of the upper cabinetry. What's more, the usual shortcomings of metal on a countertop—namely, that it's clattery and cold to the touch—are irrelevant on a vertical plane. Metal sheeting is a bit more difficult to source, however; the typical tile showroom won't show much in the way of stainless, let alone other metallics. Restaurant supply stores, often a relatively inexpensive option, can custom-fabricate metal backsplashes to your measurements and in a variety of finishes: smooth, hammered, ribbed, or even quilted, like a 1950s diner. Perfect with a stainless countertop, naturally, metal backsplashes also look great with just about any smooth, sleek surface. They can enliven Corian or bring a cutting edge to a veined stone like marble.

Wood and Wainscoting

Would you, could you . . . consider wood? Plenty of people like the look of bead board; it has a classic country charm and costs a fraction of the price of tile or stone. There is a catch, however.

Whether bead board (or wainscot—the terms are used interchangeably), teak, or maple, wood is not naturally water-repellent. Use it sparingly behind the sink, as repeated splashes have the tendency to swell, warp, even crack the boards. To make the wood as durable as possible, paint it with an exterior or marine-grade paint. For a variation on the bead-board theme, you can flip the boards over and nail them up on the other side. This creates what's called a *V-groove board*—both wider and deeper than the traditional narrow bead board. It's a good, strong look—but keep an eye on those grooves, where grime has a habit of setting up residence. *V-groove* looks great painted a glossy white, which makes it an ideal partner for white stones and solid counter surfaces with white markings. Beware mixing and matching with a tile countertop or a stone with strong linear markings, however; too many intersecting and conflicting lines can have a chaotic effect.

The Flooring

Does any room get more foot traffic than the kitchen? Doubtful. People are constantly traipsing through, schlepping in groceries, grabbing a drink from the fridge, washing up at the sink. The kitchen is a natural intersection in the house, the spot where everyone congregates—to cook, eat, or just catch up on the day. With all this activity, the kitchen floor is bound to take plenty of abuse, so it must be up to the task; it must be durable, comfortable, easy to keep clean, and slip-proof.

Of course, any surface underfoot should also please your appetite for good design. You may like the look of tile or stone in the European manner, the retro appeal of sheet vinyl or linoleum, or the comfortable, chic, and ecologically conscious cork. Or you may want wood, plain and simple—or not so simple. Since wood has had a resurgence in popularity, beginning in the early nineties, the choices have grown dramatically—in part because of the emergence of durable polyurethane coatings and in part because of the availability of many species of wood, traditional and exotic.

[ABOVE] TERRA-COTTA FLOOR TILES CREATE A WARM, RUSTIC LOOK AND DON'T SHOW MUCH DIRT. IN TERMS OF MAINTENANCE, YOU CAN LET THEM AGE NATURALLY (AND CHARMINGLY, AS HERE) OR WAX THEM REGULARLY FOR AN EVEN LUSTER.

[ABOVE LEFT] A RENOVATION OFTEN TURNS INTO AN EXCAVATION. CERAMIC TILE WAS REMOVED FROM THIS VINTAGE ONLY TO FIND A LAYER (OR TWO) OF WELL-ADHERED VINYL AND ROTTEN SUBFLOOR BENEATH.

[ABOVE RIGHT] THE APPEAL OF WELL-WORN PINE: LOW-MAINTENANCE. SAND, DINGS, AND DUST ARE NON-ISSUES WHEN THE FLOOR HAS THE PATINA OF OLD.

[OPPOSITE] MIXED SURFACES TO THE MAX. ORIGINAL WOOD CABINETS, A NEW BEAD-BOARD BACKSPLASH, AND STAINLESS-STEEL COUNTERTOPS PARTNER WELL WITH THE ORIGINAL OAK WOOD FLOORING.

As part of the whole visual picture, you should consider how the floor will integrate with the other surfaces in the kitchen—the countertops, walls, and cabinets. While you don't necessarily need or want all the colors and textures in the room to be the same (limestone floors and counters with neutral-toned walls and cabinets would be monotonous—vanilla to the extreme), you also don't want competing finishes to clash. A battle of swirling wood grains, for example, can give a person a migraine. A wood floor can complement a wood cabinet when the woods are in sync—when they mimic each other as closely as possible. A quartersawn wood floor, with its tight grain, closely replicates an alder or walnut cabinet. The combination of wood floors and wood cabinets, however, means you definitely need to declare an embargo on wood elsewhere in the kitchen. Even a wood breakfast room table means you're going to be awfully woody. The best tactic with woods, with all that grain, patina, movement, and motion, is to keep the rest of the kitchen, especially the counters, clean and simple.

Wood in All Its Variations

Wood is a natural for floors. It's strong and sturdy, with just enough give that a dropped plate might bounce off it rather than shatter into pieces. Visually, a wood's grain acts as a camouflage, hiding everyday wear and tear (crumbs of food, specks of dirt, even the occasional

scratch or nick). And wood endures forever—with a little refurbishing. It can be sanded, stained, and buffed time and again to look like new. To my mind, wood only becomes more exquisite as it ages and softens with time and use. Perhaps the real beauty of wood is its ability to tap our emotion. When you walk into a kitchen with a wood floor, you get a feeling of warmth, of comfort, of coming home.

The wonderful attributes and familiarity of wood don't make the choice of *which* particular wood to lay down any easier. Countless species (to say nothing of engineered and prefinished woods) exist in a multitude of sizes and finishes. The best approach is to picture the whole sweep of your kitchen floor and then get down to the pragmatics—the nitty-gritty of money and maintenance.

Oak accounts for 90 percent of all hardwood installations—and logically so, given that it's affordable and many homes already have oak floors in other rooms. It's a natural instinct to bring the wood floor into the kitchen to match.

The first decision is white or red—and we're talking wood, not wine. White oak has ash tones, whereas red oak has a pinkish, salmon cast. These undertones will radiate through most stain finishes, affecting the way the oak looks as a finished entity. Speaking of stains, oaks accept them gracefully, whether pickled (white), ebony (greenish black), mahogany (redder-toned brown), walnut (warm, lighter brown), or golden.

As for the size of the strips, oak, like many other species, is generally sold in a mixed bundle of lengths from 1 to 7 feet, and in an average width of 2¼ inches. But oak is also readily available in wider planks, up to 5 inches, at a minimal increase in cost. I say, why not go wide? In my opinion, matching the width of the planks in the kitchen to the rest of the house isn't always easy or even advisable. For one thing, the existing floors of the house are likely to be and look older. For another, laying down wider planks in the kitchen can be a welcome change of pace, making the space appear less busy (fewer strips) while maintaining a cohesiveness with the rest of the house.

Wood is cut in one of two ways. Plainsawn, the most common and least costly, has a distinctive wavy grain known as cathedraling (like a church spire). Quartersawn, in which the wood is cut across the grain, requires a technique that takes more work and creates a little more waste—hence, the higher cost. The payback of a quartersawn floor is a beautiful, straight pattern that makes for a surface that's more stable and less prone to the expansion and contraction typical of the wavy plainsawn variety.

Maple and birch are close in character—light-hued, close-grained, and even-textured. They're also hard, with a uniform surface—a reason they're often laid down in gyms. Maple and birch are so hard, in fact, that most common stains don't penetrate the surface. Dark hues look muddy, so it's better to stay on the light side. More pricy than oak, these woods are also more prone to swell or buckle when they encounter water—less than optimal in the kitchen.

Mahogany, with its dark, reddish-brown hue and undulating grain often flecked with red, is dramatic. It's also durable and practical because it resists both moisture and dents. Mahogany's

[ABOVE] THIS CAPACIOUS ISLAND HOUSES A COOKTOP, A BAR SINK, AND CLEVER AMENITIES SUCH AS CUSTOM PULLOUT PILASTERS TO STORE SPICES AND CONDIMENTS, BUT IT'S THE ISLAND'S EXOTIC SURFACE—WALNUT WITH AFRICAN MAHOGANY BANDING AND CORNERSTONES—THAT NEARLY STEALS THE SHOW.

[OPPOSITE] JUST BECAUSE YOU MOVE—OR RENOVATE—MORE THAN ONCE (IN THIS FAMILY'S CASE, THREE TIMES IN SIX YEARS), DON'T FEEL LIKE YOU HAVE TO REINVENT THE WHEEL EACH TIME. IF A PARTICULAR APPLIANCE WORKS FOR YOUR FAMILY, STICK TO YOUR STYLE GUNS.

TRACKING A WOOD FLOOR FROM START TO FINISH: A TYPICAL TIMELINE

- Pick species of wood.
- Install subfloor.
- Accept delivery of flooring—from a week to a month after ordering.
- Allow planks to acclimate to the home's environment for a period of several days to several weeks.
- Lay floor.
- Sand floor and then cover with a heavy paper, called *rosin paper,* to protect it from dirt and grit while the rest of the kitchen renovation takes place.
- Lightly sand or screen prior to staining.
- Apply stain of choice.
- Finish with two or more coats of polyurethane (either oil- or water-based) for protection.
- Cover freshly stained floor with paper (being careful not to adhere tape directly to floor but rather to casings and base moldings) and allow to cure for three or four days (for water-based poly) or up to a month (for oil-based poly). Curing hardens the finish, making it more impervious to pets' claws, soccer cleats, and so on.

[MAPLE]

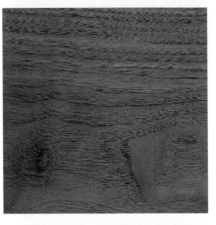

[WALNUT]

[CHERRY TRIM]

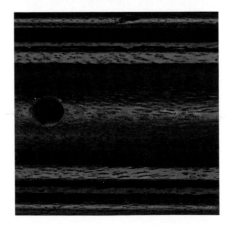

[MAHOGANY TRIM]

[PINE]

[BIRCH]

[OAK]

[CORK]

fine texture also takes finish well. However, because it's a relatively rare wood, it's priced accordingly.

Walnut ranges from a deep, rich brown to a purplish black. It has a consistent grain and accepts stain finishes easily, especially deep, ebonized hues. Of the several varieties of walnut, Brazilian is the strongest and most kitchenworthy—not so American walnut, which tends to be too soft for a kitchen.

Pine is probably the most pedestrian of all woods, but it covers a lot of territory in style and price. Be sure you know what type you're buying before you have it cut to fit. The least costly of the lot, yellow pine, is also the least practical. It's so soft that furniture and heels can dig into the surface. Heart pine (usually redder in tone) is a step up in hardness and price. Pine can even shoot into the high-end category with a type known as river-recovered—logs that have sunk and been preserved underwater, giving them a rare and rich old-growth patina.

Cherry ranks as one of the richest woods, in hues from deep orange to reddish brown, often with dramatic streaks. Falling in the middle of the price spectrum, cherry has a subtle, almost unseen grain. Like oak, cherry can be specified either plainsawn or quartersawn. It takes a variety of stains well but oxidizes a lot, which means it is prone to darkening more dramatically than other woods over time.

Staining the Grains

Wood is naked until it's finished with a coat or two of stain. Even if you choose to leave it in the buff, a floor needs a top coat of clear sealant. To get an idea of your color options, consult a stain chart. This will help you narrow your many choices to a handful of candidates.

Next step: Get some samples down on your floor. You don't want to simply pick Special Walnut or English Chestnut from the chart, only to be disappointed that your finished floors bear little resemblance to the postage-stamp-size sample. When you request the stain samples, don't just rattle off the numbers or the names. Describe to the finisher or the paint store salesperson the qualities you are looking for—a warm brown floor without too much red, for instance, or a yellowish brown, or a black brown. This will allow them to recommend other options or to tell you if the ones you've chosen will give you the results you're looking for.

At both extremes of the color spectrum are a couple of points to keep in mind. White finishes can show cracks between boards (they appear as thin black lines), especially if expansion and contraction occurs. With ebony or other very dark hues, dust, scratches, and water spots are highly visible.

When the samples are applied to the kitchen floor, don't walk away while they dry. Make sure you see and assess the stains while they're still wet; that's what they'll look like after they've been polyurethaned. A sample that's already dried looks like just that—dried out. You may actually find that you want to experiment on the spot by mixing a stain or two together to get a richer, more nuanced color. (Take care not to shake the finishes as you would a paint, which causes bubbles. Stir from the bottom up.) Be prepared with cups or empty coffee cans in which to mix stains. Keep in mind that stain mixing is an art, not a science. You or your finisher may have to try several combinations to get the exact hue you're after. Patience in this process almost always pays off.

Once you've made your choice and applied the final color and let it dry, it's time to top it off with a sealer. Oil-based polyurethane, the traditional choice, goes on clear, imparting a rich glow, but it can yellow over time. The newer water-based polyurethanes (one of my favorites is Bonakemi Traffic) cost a little more but dry more quickly—in two to three hours versus eight or more for the oil-based variety. Water-based polys also tend to cast a slight haze over the stain, affecting the luster ever so subtly.

[BELOW] SAMPLES OF LINOLEUM.

TRADE TIP

While polyurethane manufacturers claim their products dry within hours, it takes longer for them to fully cure. Water-based polys cure in three or four days. Oil-based polys can take a whopping thirty days to cure completely. To allow the floor the air it needs to dry, wait the full curing time before moving in furniture or throwing down area rugs.

As a final step, some people like to wax and buff their kitchen floors. This creates a soft, polished, but not shiny look—as well as a little extra protection. Be aware, however, that waxing is a commitment. You need to apply the wax with a sponge mop bimonthly to keep the finish smooth, and you must be careful to wipe up wet areas promptly or you risk getting white marks (like the telltale ring a glass leaves on a wood table).

Factory Flooring

If you don't have the time or inclination to go through all the steps and decisions involved in laying a custom-made wood floor, you have the option of ordering a ready-made floor that can be installed right out of the box. There are three categories within the factory-made genre: prefinished, engineered, and laminate.

Prefinished floors, made from hardwood—ash to walnut— are stained and sealed at the factory with four coats. The advantage to a factory floor: There's no guesswork. You know what you are getting. There's also little mess in installation—no dust created by sanding, no chemical fumes, and no random bits preserved in the finish, all risks with traditional wood floors that are finished on site. With prefinished floors, all imperfections in the final finishing are eliminated. Prefinished floors also have additives that help the flooring resist abrasion, moisture, and even UV rays. One timing issue to factor in: You can't lay prefin-

FIELD NOTE

Decorator Kat Burki is lucky enough to live in a home that dates from the 1700s. When she moved in six years ago, however, the flooring was standard-issue and bland—what she called 1970s Colonial. From a local wood supplier, Kat found reclaimed pine floorboards measuring a good 12 inches wide. (I'm not sure we let our trees grow old enough these days to yield foot-wide boards!) As for the floor's finish, she mixed her own and stopped at a color she describes as "near chest-nut." When it came time to seal the flooring, Kat eschewed polyurethane—a brave move. She can't stand the way it builds up and thinks poly turns plasticky and orangey over time. Instead, she had her floors finished with paste wax, which adds a transparent layer of protection, and has had no slipping problems whatsoever—except, that is, on the stairs. After a few sleigh rides down the stairs, Kat added carpet.

TRADE TIP

Wood's enemies are water and grit. Don't leave spills for long periods, or you risk warping. Sweep sandy material right away so shoes won't crunch it into the finish. Other than that, wood floors are a breeze to maintain. Basic vacuuming and damp mopping should keep them looking buff for years.

TRADE TIP

As floorboards usually run lengthwise through a room—to direct and guide you through the space—you want to place a saddle perpendicular to the surrounding flooring. This change of direction has another advantage: It helps mitigate any disparity between generations of woods.

ished floors until everything else in the kitchen is done lest the new floor be splattered by paint or scratched by appliances being installed. (This isn't a problem with traditional wood floors, which tend to be installed early and then covered; even so, small scratches are inevitable and are taken care of with a light final screening sanding and final coat of polyurethane.) These floors are a bit more expensive than traditional floor installations, and wood grain choices and width sizes are more limited. But convenience, not cost, tends to attract homeowners to this flooring option.

So-called **engineered floors** are also factory-finished, but each plank, instead of being solid through and through, consists of a series of thin layers or plies that are glued together and topped with a veneer of hardwood. The top wood is the premium wood (underlayers are less expensive and more readily available plies of wood), which generally means a lower price point for this flooring compared to solid wood floors. The multi-ply construction of engineered flooring has other benefits, too. It creates a surface that's more stable than regular wood, which makes it a good choice for damp locales or places with extreme swings of humidity. And these floors can be glued down or allowed to float over any subsurface: cement, vinyl, existing wood. The floating floor clips together over a foam pad (so it doesn't clap against the subfloor) and requires no nails. The veneer looks so good you'd be hard pressed to tell the difference between an engineered floor and a regular one. The thinner top layer means a shorter lifespan, however; unlike real wood, you can refinish a veneer just once or twice in its lifetime.

Another in-the-box variation is **laminate flooring.** The word *laminate* is usually paired with *countertop,* but laminate makes a perfectly legitimate flooring material, too. When used as flooring, laminate is fabricated in a different manner and typically fashioned to look like real wood. Planks made of fiberboard are topped with a hyperrealistic photographic image of a wood species. Choices in faux grains range from hickory to the more exotic African species called zebrawood. The photo image is actually glued to the face of the board and protected by a strong, clear coat of poly. Like its countertop counterpart, laminate flooring is strong, scratch-resistant, and affordable (laminate flooring runs in the low range of a real wood floor). The flooring also shares the downside of a laminate counter: If and when the surface gets nicked, the damage, unfortunately, is irreparable.

[ABOVE] CHARCOAL SLATE FLOORING, ONCE THE EXCLUSIVE DOMAIN OF SUNROOMS AND MUDROOMS, IS WELL-SUITED TO KITCHENS AS WELL. DARK FLOORS DO SHOW DUST, BUT THEY CAMOUFLAGE DIRT FROM DOG PAWS AND SOCCER CLEATS.

[OPPOSITE] THE REAL DEAL: OAK PLANK FLOORING STAINED A WARM TONE LIKE THIS 50/50 COMBINATION OF MINWAX'S PROVINCIAL AND GOLDEN OAK CAN BE RESTAINED OR REPOLYURETHANED OVER THE YEARS.

A whitewashed floor is far from one-note. It can show up in a number of shades and subtleties, depending on the staining process. Just remember that regardless of the finish you use, white has a habit of turning dark in the fine separation between the boards.

Pickling involves coating the wood with a semi-opaque stain (like those from the companies Minwax and Behr). The finished effect is more of a pale gray, or even a slight pink, than a true white, but the overall hue is unmistakably light. The semi-opaque quality of the pickling stain makes this technique particularly suited to a floor with a lot of imperfections; it also helps visually unify mismatched generations of woods. If your floor is old and separating or your foundation is not solid and your floorboards not flush tight, the cracks and spaces between the boards will show up as black lines.

Liming gives floors a matte, almost chalky appearance. An acid-based substance, liming is applied as a wax and dries to a muted gray-white that helps mask the yellow or red tones on the wood's surface.

Bleaching works aggressively by opening the grain of a wood floor so it takes color easily. Much like fabric bleach, floor bleach is strong stuff, not to be used lightly. It tends to weaken wood fibers, making floors more vulnerable to wear and tear. It's perhaps best reserved for existing flooring already in dubious condition.

TRANSITION PIECES

Inevitably, it seems, the kitchen floor height is different from that of the adjacent rooms, whether due to the settling of the house or simply a difference in depth between neighboring surfaces. Fortunately, you can graciously and ergonomically bridge the gaps with reducer saddles. These saddles, typically fashioned from a solid piece of oak, span the width of the door and can be either single or double ramped, meaning one or both sides slope from low to high, easing the transition and reducing the chances of tripping. It's important to match the saddle's wood—oak with oak; cherry with cherry—or at least have the saddle stained in a similar or matching finish. If the height differential between two rooms is more than 1 inch, you may need to extend the saddle beyond the doorjamb a bit; the additional length allows the ramp to rise more gently. This kind of attention to detail makes for a graceful transition from one space to the next.

Earthy Surfaces: Stone to Tile

"Hard as a rock" is a good thing when it comes to floors. Granite, slate, ceramic tile, even cement are all tough contenders for a kitchen. Unlike a kitchen counter, where the preference for high polish or honing is a personal one, a highly polished floor is slippery and dangerous. Stay with low-sheen or slightly gritty stones that offer some grip.

Without a doubt, stone is elegant. It's also cold on the toes and vulnerable to cracks if something hard or heavy is dropped on the surface. And stone is expensive. Fortunately, with more and more of it being quarried every year, supply is matching demand, and the cost is slowly decreasing.

Unlike countertop stone choices, which are seemingly boundless, stone used for flooring must be especially long-lasting. The hardest stones—granite and quartzite—are the most indestructible. Limestones and marbles are more porous and therefore more apt to stain than the harder stones, but they, too, will last forever. Think of the marble steps of Versailles—700 years old and still intact. Harvested from an old European chateau, reclaimed stone flooring has a certain allure, but I find it impractical, not to mention exorbitantly expensive, to use in a large area. These stones are frequently uneven and require much manipulation and coddling on installation. In this case, mellow new stones trump the legitimate antique.

As important as patina is, the stone's size and the pattern in which it is laid dramatically affect the look of the space. On the macro scale, the bigger the stone, the more expansive the floor will seem—that means, somewhat counterintuitively, that oversized stones can make a small space appear more spacious. Very large kitchens may incorporate more than one size of stone—a field of

TRADE TIP

Stone is heavy. A 1-foot cube of granite, for instance, tops the scales at nearly 200 pounds. Be sure—before any mortar is set!—that your subfloor can carry the load. If the substrate is not rigid enough, the stone pieces may crack.

[ABOVE] SOME SLATES ARE HEARTIER THAN OTHERS. HERE, THE OWNERS CHOSE A GOOD-QUALITY TYPE CALLED CHINA LOTUS. SUBSEQUENT SEALING FURTHER PROTECTS THE STONE FROM CHIPS AND WATER DAMAGE.

[ABOVE] MORE-THAN-CENTURY-OLD CONCRETE HAS STOOD THE TEST OF TIME. A STYLISH STENCIL BRINGS IT UP TO DATE.

TRADE TIP

Hydronic heat is installed with no nails—and for good reason. Those water-filled plastic and rubber coils can be punctured. While installing a door stop in one home, the carpenter inadvertently nailed into the floor and sprung a geyser. It was expensive to get the heating system repaired.

square pieces in the center, for instance, with a border of smaller stones. Generally speaking, a diagonally repeated pattern enlarges a space, while a staggered joint (a running bond or brick pattern) leads you to and through a space. In most instances, you'll want to avoid an entire floor made up of small stones; all those grout lines will contribute to a very busy effect.

How the stones are finished is a matter of both preference and practicality. Polished stones, while glossy and glamorous, tend to be slippery—and, what's more, the polish wears off in the more trafficked areas, leaving the floor looking unbalanced. A honed stone, on the other hand, wears beautifully and evenly.

Slate, the renowned outdoor-indoor surface, is chic but tricky. Richly textured but naturally brittle, slate is more apt to fissure over time than harder stones. From a style point of view, there is a lot of variation in the slate family. Slate can be ordered either clefted (with rough striations) or unclefted (tumbled and smooth), and in a range of colors from subtle green to verging-on-murky brown. Most showrooms will hand-select the most handsome and even-hued slate for display. To ensure that you get the earth tones you want (more gray-green, for instance, and less pond-scum green), ask to see all the possible color variations before you order.

Quartzite is more durable than slate and even less expensive. This stone's color palette tends to be warm—golds, browns, and ivories—and pieces are typically flecked with bits of silver mica. While some renovators embrace quartzite's reasonable price and rustic charm, its rough texture proves too tactile for most in the kitchen.

Concrete, despite its industrial associations, can actually be soft-looking and buffed to a lustrous sheen. While standard-issue concrete has a gray industrial cast, the finish can be manipulated in a number of ways. For example, you can have integral color added to the material to make it a uniform shade through and through, swirl in powdered masonry colorants for a variegated look, paint and stencil bare concrete for a decorative effect, or have it scored or stamped into patterns.

Far less expensive than stone, concrete is hardy stuff. It's also relatively easy to put down (easier, certainly, than pulling it up). In a typical installation, concrete is poured on site, right on top of metal reinforcing bars or mesh (it's a heavy material, remember) and then allowed to set . . . and set . . . and set. A quirk of installation: Concrete takes a full thirty days to cure. That's thirty days when nothing else can happen in the kitchen—no painter finishing the walls, no plumber hooking up the sink, no family cooking, nada.

FIELD NOTE

Leah Mullin chose a polished limestone for her renovated kitchen in a 1940s home in northwest Atlanta, but when she had laid just a few pieces, she deemed the surface too slick. The offending pieces were pulled up, and she was faced with the decision of where to go from there. For inspiration, her contractor looked no farther than the backyard. He suggested that she run the same crab orchard stone, a muted taupe brown stone indigenous to the area and used on the terrace, right into the kitchen. Leah was worried, though, that the rough texture would be a problem for the barefooted. They experimented with several pieces, sanding them onsite to yield a smoother texture. In the process, Leah discovered that sanding transformed the rustic stone's color as well, turning it a warmer, lighter color—less gray-brown and more gray-gold. To set the kitchen apart from the neighboring terrace, the sanded stones were laid diagonally and finished with several coats of sealer to lend a warm and welcoming patina.

WARM UNDERFOOT

As its name implies, radiant heat radiates from the floor, invisibly and evenly. It replaces the need for baseboard or radiator units, eliminating visual clutter, noise, and some allergens, which normally enter a house through vents and ducts.

Radiant systems can be hydronic or electric. With hydronic, the more common method, the system runs right off the boiler. The boiler heats water that is carried via a network of tubes encased in concrete. This concrete layer becomes the base, or subfloor, for the finished floor material, be it tile, stone, or wood, which floats (no nails anchor it) above. (Factor this into your overall plan: Thermal tubes raise the floor height by about ½ inch. Added to the depth of the cement and the top flooring, the total difference can amount to a hefty step between adjacent rooms.) Once you've paid—and handsomely so—for the installation, radiant heat usually ends up saving you money; it's 20 to 30 percent more efficient (and therefore more environmentally correct) than forced air heating. After all, you've already got a boiler (or are adding one, for new construction). Hydronic heat is controlled with a thermostat, making it easy to regulate. It does, however, take a while to heat the whole room.

Electric radiance, while less expensive to install, is considerably more expensive to run. It comes from loops of narrow electrical wires; no concrete is required. Because of its thinness, an electric network of wires can be laid anywhere in the house, but it is best reserved for small spots (like bathrooms, not kitchens) to keep your electric bills in line. Electric radiance is not as efficient or as effective as hydronic. It would be unwise to try to heat a suburban home with electric radiance.

Ceramic tile is the most hard-wearing and impenetrable of all flooring materials—something people have known for thousands of years, judging by the longevity of tile's popularity. Made from ingredients of the earth—one reason for its ancient roots—ceramic tile comprises mixed clays and other minerals that are shaped and fired at very high temperatures to form a hard body. Like any batter, the longer and hotter you bake the mixture (called a bisque), the denser and more impervious it gets. Of course, any tile can crack or break if you drop a heavy enough object on it from a great enough distance. Still, my experience is that if your foundation is secure, it's rare to see a fault line running across the floor. If there is a crack, it's usually in the joints or seams. When it comes to the kitchen floor, obviously, the harder and more impermeable, the better.

Once the bisque is formed and fired, it may be left untreated or finished with some form of glaze. A glaze is typically made of colored glass (hundreds and hundreds of shades are available) that's fused to the bisque under intense heat. The glaze renders the bisque stain-resistant (non-porous), which means it does not need resealing. As appealing as that sounds, glaze tends to wear off in high traffic areas and can become slippery on floors. Make sure the tile you like is rated as suitable for flooring, as many highly glazed ceramics are intended for walls or light traffic only.

An emerging category of glazed flooring tiles, made of either ceramic or the even harder-

[ABOVE] CRAB ORCHARD, A STONE INDIGENOUS TO THE AREA, WAS RUN BOTH INDOORS AND OUT IN THIS GEORGIA HOME. INSIDE IT WAS HAND-SANDED TO REMOVE ROUGH EDGES AND CREATE A SMOOTHER SURFACE. SURPRISE, SURPRISE—THE SANDING TURNED THE STONE A SOFTER, MORE PLEASING COLOR, BETTER SUITED TO AN INTERIOR.

wearing porcelain, has the mellow sheen of true stone. As they say, imitation is the highest form of flattery. While some imitations are unmistakably faux, others are so skillful that they fool you. Almost. As good as the pretenders are, none can truly mimic the irregularity in color and markings of the real thing. The price is right, however, and if cost is a factor, it pays to look into one of the great pretenders as an alternative to real stone.

As for tiles in the unglazed grouping, the best known is earthen-red terra-cotta. Also called quarry tile, terra-cotta tiles are made from pieces of clay that have been baked in the sun or the kiln and left au naturel. Terra-cotta is naturally thicker and denser than glazed tiles, though its palette is narrow—variations on peaches, oranges, and rusts. I have installed terra-cotta in two of our family's kitchens over the years, and I find the floor tiles share certain qualities with good wine—they improve with age. Over time (and with multiple waxings), terra-cotta takes on a mellow and warm patina.

The Alternatives

Wood and tile are certainly the two classic choices for a kitchen floor, but they're hardly the only options. Whether you're looking for a floor that's eco-conscious, exotic-looking, or a little offbeat, there's a surface to suit.

Bamboo sounds, on the face of it, implausible as a floor. You'd think it would be bumpy and brittle. Not at all. Bamboo is perfectly smooth and quite durable, with very little grain or pattern. While it's technically a woody grass, as flooring, bamboo is a natural blonde and actually harder than maple or oak and less prone to contracting and expanding.

The transition from plant to flooring goes like this: The stalks are first milled into strips. Next, three layers of the grass are laminated under high pressure to create planks. (Bamboo needs three coats of acrylic urethane to make the surface strong and resistant to water and mildew.) The planks are then assembled as tongue-in-groove boards and ready to be shipped and laid down like regular wood. Bamboo is generally available in the same

[LEFT] A CLASSIC UNDERFOOT CHOICE: WARM WOOD FLOORING BLENDS WITH A VARIETY OF WOODEN AND WOVEN FURNISHINGS.

BETWEEN THE TILES

Decisions about grout are often an afterthought, but grout actually has a pretty important job to do. It bonds tiles together, which helps prevent cracks, and it keeps water away from the substrate, which helps prevent warping and rot. Of course, grout is best known for its flaws, namely its tendency to collect dirt and grime in its crevices. To make grout less prone to staining, have it sealed after installation (allowing it to cure for several days first) and then resealed every few years thereafter.

As for the color of the grout, it's often a surprise to renovators that they have a choice—in fact, many choices. A high-contrast grout (either dramatically lighter or darker than the tile itself) makes the tile pattern appear bolder. If the grout blends with the tile, the pattern is subtler and can even fade to the point of looking like a continuous surface. Personally, I like grout to be grout-colored—that is, grayish, pewterish, or stone-ish—rather than some unnatural blue, green, or yellow.

widths and lengths as regular hardwood, though it is available only as prefinished boards.

Exotic appeal aside, bamboo has the advantage of being completely eco-friendly. Because the stalks are trimmed rather than cut down, we're talking about an infinitely renewable and sustainable resource.

Cork tiles are made from none other than cork trees. If you ever read *Ferdinand* to your kids, you'll remember the lazy Spanish bull who'd rather sleep under a cork tree than go into the bullfight. The tiles are manufactured from renewable bark that's harvested from cork trees, a type of oak found in the Mediterranean. The trees are never cut down and their habitat is undisturbed, making cork a true eco-friendly choice.

Less expensive than many other ecology-minded alternatives, cork has a lot going for it, both practically and aesthetically. I first discovered cork as a flooring in an 1890s mansion in New York City. It astounded me. The cork was not only intact but in good condition. Clearly, it's resilient, but cork is also cushiony and soundproof—sound-*deadening*, in fact (the reason old-time recording studios were cork-lined). When properly sealed, cork is even water-repellent. It's also easy to maintain: A coat of wax (atop the polyurethane sealer) will prolong the time between resealing, which is recommended every three years or so and keeps the cork looking matte. And because cork comes in tiles or planks (typical sizes are 12 by 12, 12 by 24, or 24 by 24 inches), repair is simple—a single cracked or stained tile can be popped out and replaced as needed, even by a nonpro. No grout is required; the tiles just butt up against one another.

As attractive as cork sounds, it's not impervious to criticism; because it's so soft, heavy furniture can leave permanent impressions, though cork rebounds nicely from regular day-to-day activity. During the nascent days of the resurgence of cork as a popular flooring choice, it came in a range of colors from aqua to milky white. For the most part, these fashion hues have been dropped by manufacturers, and most corks are either honey (light) or pecan (dark) in color. Regardless of the hue, cork's natural mottled, freckled pattern hides damage and dings. (See the photograph on page 149.)

Linoleum, first patented in 1863, was a favorite in kitchens and baths from its inception, but it fell out of

TRADE TIP

Tiles that are crazed or crackled—a special glazing process that deliberately leaves fine cracks visible in the tile—are just as strong and water-resistant as those with a uniform surface.

[ABOVE] IF YOU'RE GOING WITH TILE, MAKE SURE TO ORDER PLENTY OF EXTRA PIECES. WHILE IT'S EASY TO POP OUT A BROKEN TILE AND REPLACE IT, IT'S NOT ALWAYS SO EASY TO GET ONE THAT MATCHES YOUR ORIGINAL IN HUE (EVEN WHITE HAS MANY VARIATIONS).

[ABOVE] A CLASSIC CHECKERBOARD, HERE IN RED AND WHITE VINYL, BRIGHTENS UP A BRAND-NEW LAMINATE KITCHEN.

[OPPOSITE] HERE BLACK AND WHITE CERAMIC TILE (BOTH IN AN 8-INCH SQUARE) MODERNIZES ORIGINAL PAINTED WOOD CABINETS. A THICK CORIAN COUNTERTOP FURTHERS THE LOOK.

fashion in the 1970s when vinyl came along. But linoleum is bouncing back, and in this eco-conscious environment, it has a lot of appeal. Made from a combination of linseed oil, powdered cork or wood, ground limestone, and resins, and backed with jute fiber, it's 100 percent natural. The one well-known down side of linoleum—that it is impossible to repair once damaged—has been mitigated with durable presealed tiles and sheets. Some manufacturers, such as Marmoleum, even incorporate an antistatic feature and the increasingly popular antimicrobial protection. While the retro look isn't right for every kitchen, linoleum is available in so many vibrant hues, marbled or solid, it's quite clear this is not your grandmother's flooring.

Vinyl, a decidedly less natural flooring option, is often confused with linoleum, but the difference lies in vinyl's durability (less) and price (also less). Made from petroleum-based polyvinyl chloride (PVC) and available as either sheets or vinyl composite tiles, vinyl can be a great choice, especially in a vintage kitchen. A checkerboard pattern of tiles with flecks of color always looks fresh, though remember that vinyl doesn't have much real estate cachet and likely won't add to the resale value of a renovated kitchen.

Whatever the final choice, once you've looked at the surface options for your floors and counters, you'll not only be informed, you'll be inspired.

The Lighting

Lighting is an essential ingredient in a successful kitchen, yet we tend to think and talk about it far less than other kitchen decisions. Not many people walk into a kitchen and exclaim, "What great lighting you have!" But believe me, good (and bad) lighting registers, even if it's at the subliminal level. Lighting sets the tone of the space, injecting it with energy and vitality. Of course, lighting also illuminates a kitchen, so you can see clearly when chopping, cooking, and cleaning up. Done well, lighting can even flatter the people seated around the table.

You could say that lighting plays a bigger role in the kitchen than in any other room. Nowhere else in the home do we use as much electricity—25 percent or more of our entire household consumption is taken up by kitchen appliances and lights, which burn, on average, twice as long as any other lights in the house (and that statistic holds true in both urban and suburban settings). True, the sheer size of a kitchen accounts for some of this megawattage, but function also plays a part. Think about it: What harm can come of a dim living room? Not much! But in a kitchen, you're wielding knives and carrying pots of scalding water. You need overall lighting, path lighting, task lighting, undercounter lighting, recessed lighting, surface-mounted lighting, not to mention evanescent lighting for atmosphere.

The appeal of multiple light sources certainly plays out in my own ninety-year-old, light-laden kitchen, which has three hanging pendants (one a double), three recessed low voltage halogens, a surface-mounted fixture, numerous undercabinet fluorescents, and five lamps—not to mention a bank of east-facing windows. Together, these light sources emit a lush, layered luminosity.

Best of all, I can control the intensity of the light with dimmers, which I've installed on every switch except the undercounter lights (fluorescents aren't available with dimmers). In addition to the dimmable overhead lighting, I have several tabletop lamps in which I've put three-way bulbs to allow for adjustable brightness. By varying the combinations of light intensity, I am able to create just the right amount of task or mood lighting. By day, with sunlight streaming in and a few lights turned on, the kitchen is bright and functioning at full speed—with plenty of brightness for slicing a bagel, checking e-mail, or making lunch. In the evening, with all the lights dimmed and the undercounter fluorescents turned off, the room

[OPPOSITE] A WELL-LIT ROOM HAS MULTIPLE LIGHT SOURCES IN A VARIETY OF FORMS AND SHAPES. THIS KITCHEN DOES IT PERFECTLY, PAIRING UNDERCOUNTER LIGHTS WITH RECESSED HIGH HATS ON THE EXTERIOR PERIMETER AND BELL LANTERNS WITH LAMPS, TOPPING IT ALL OFF WITH A HANGING PENDANT.

becomes a cozy gathering place for the family or an inviting setting for entertaining guests.

The lighting you choose for your kitchen will have a dramatic effect on the room's look and feel. The fixtures, bulbs, and locations of the lights themselves can all influence the perception of space—making a room appear bigger or more intimate. Too much brightness can make a kitchen feel lab-like and cast an unflattering light over everything. Too little, and you're constantly bemoaning the lack of adequate illumination to cook and clean up. Lighting is tricky, and many people are understandably intimidated by it. But once you understand the basics of placement, wattage, and wiring, you'll be able to approach the task of lighting your kitchen with clarity.

Capturing the Daylight

You can't really talk about lighting choices without accounting for natural light—invited in via windows, skylights, or French doors. I have never heard a customer complain about too much natural light in a kitchen! Early in the construction or renovation process, it's a good idea to determine how much daylight your kitchen gets (and what type—morning or afternoon) and how you will need to augment it. Speak with the contractor or architect about potential places to install new windows or enlarge existing ones. Whether you're changing the perimeter of a kitchen by expanding or working within the confines of the existing space, adding windows or French doors is often a reasonable proposition, especially compared to the cost of cabinetry or appliances.

My kitchen originally had only two small windows on one wall, separated by dark and clunky upper cabinets. The cabinetry dwarfed the undersized windows and cut down the meager light. By taking out both windows and the interrupting cabinetry, I created room to install an 8-foot-long expanse of glass with crank-out casements at each end (infinitely easier to open than double-hung windows, especially when reaching up and over base cabinets). Yes, this resulted in fewer upper cabinets, but it was a small sacrifice to make. The formerly gloomy space now frames a sweeping view to the lawn.

Similarly, a kitchen can be opened up by placing two windows side by side (rather than separated), creating one large expanse of eye-catching glass and a generous slice of light, or by aligning windows with doorways so that, as you enter and look out, your eye takes in the breadth of the space. When reconfiguring your windows, be sure to take in the view from the outside looking in as well. Double-check that the new apertures appear rhythmic and not jarring on the exterior, especially in relationship to the existing windows and doors elsewhere in the house.

[ABOVE] AFTER A SMALL-SCALE RENOVATION: A BANK OF CABINETS CAME DOWN TO MAKE WAY FOR A BANK OF LARGE WINDOWS. I HAPPILY TRADED UPPER STORAGE FOR THE LIGHT.

[OPPOSITE] NOTHING BEATS THE NATURAL LIGHT PROVIDED BY THIS TRIO OF ATELIER-LIKE SKYLIGHTS.

Another important factor to consider in placement is the direction of the sun. East-facing windows are bathed in morning light—great if you're an early riser. West-facing glass lets in the evening sunset, which sounds romantic but comes with a caveat. In my last house, we baked while the dinner baked. It was just too, too hot in the late-day sun, and we were forced to add an awning. South-facing windows soak in the sunshine, whereas north-facing windows provide flat light and not a glimmer of sun.

You might also consider skylights, which let in a flood of light from overhead. Because they penetrate the roof, however, they can create waterproofing issues, especially if they are added after the fact to the existing roof. Be wary of the cheap bubble types, which may not only leak but can also look, well, cheap. Handsome, well-constructed skylights can be expensive. Another aesthetic issue to consider: If you have the choice of doing a pair of smallish skylights or one grand one, opt for the latter, which is more dramatic and less likely to make the ceiling appear chopped up. Some municipalities have restrictions, historical and otherwise, on skylights, particularly on the front of the house; you have a better shot at getting them approved for the rear. (A quick call to the building department in your municipality will yield a guideline regarding skylight usage.) When skylights are done well, they're magic—moving and changing with the seasons, revealing dappled light, droplets of rain, dusting snowfalls, and starry nights—all right there in your kitchen.

French doors bring with them a romantic ambiance and allow for the flow from indoor to outdoor rooms. I'm such a devotee of these doors, I believe they should at least be considered in any renovation or new project. In our house, we added three sets of French doors across the entire back of the breakfast room. The center set opens while the other two pairs are fixed, cutting down on the expense of hardware and screen doors as well as reducing drafts. You needn't confine French doors to exterior openings; you can also link two rooms or conceal a pantry, adding lightness to a space that may otherwise be floor-to-ceiling cabinetry. Curtaining the doors partway up is a way to hide the clutter.

Clean-lined, all-glass doors, whether they swing or slide, are another option for letting light (and people) into a kitchen. But because they consist of a single pane of glass, these doors may make you feel a bit exposed, whereas the mullions of French doors provide a modicum of privacy. Either way, keep in mind that glass turns black at night and can add a visual chill to the room without enough additional lighting. In fact, all the windows and doors in the world are meaningless once the sun goes down or the clouds come out. You need to be able to flip a switch or two and flood your kitchen with light.

The Art of Artificial Lighting

Although daylight enhances your kitchen when it's bright outside, it brings nothing to the dinner table, or chopping block, or message center. Artificial light is the easiest way to set a mood or completely change the atmosphere. The kitchen can segue from a bright room buzzing with prepping activity to a low-lit space set for a quiet repast—from cooking to dining.

The best lighting is perceived without necessarily being seen, and easy to adjust to the subtlest degree. While whole books are devoted to the principles of lighting design, a well-lit kitchen boils down to this generally acknowledged principle: The space should have three sources of illumination: task lighting, ambient lighting, and accent lighting. The combination of the three types provides the right amount of light for each activity and time of day, from slicing a tomato to setting the mood for dinner.

[OPPOSITE] A DARK KITCHEN ABSORBS LIGHT, WHICH IS WHY MY OWN WOOD-HEAVY SPACE NEEDED MORE ILLUMINATION THAN A WHITER, BRIGHTER KITCHEN WOULD. THESE GRACEFUL ADJUSTABLE PENDANTS (CALLED "RISE AND FALL" SINCE THEY CAN BE RAISED FOR OVERALL AMBIENCE OR LOWERED CLOSER TO COUNTERTOP FOR TASKS) HAVE MILK-GLASS GLOBES THAT MAKE THE MOST OF THEIR WATTAGE.

Task lighting, purely functional, is usually installed under the upper cabinets. Undercabinet lighting, also (illogically) known as undercounter lighting, is well suited to any job that requires bright light—especially those jobs involving knives. I like to run the task lights around the perimeter of the room—covering at least two-thirds the length of each upper cabinet—which bathes all the counters evenly. To eliminate shadows, have the lights mounted at the front, not back, edge of the cabinet's underside.

A variety of bulbs—fluorescent, halogen, xenon—can be used for undercabinet lighting. My favorite happens to be the most economical: slimline fluorescents, which create a diffuse light, last ten times longer than an average bulb, and generate no standing heat. For those who think fluorescents are unflattering, remember: These lights aren't illuminating the room or you—just your hands and the carrots you're chopping. Besides, with the new warm white fluorescent bulb options, even the carrots look good.

TRADE TIP

The number of fixtures is only part of the lighting story; wattage is the other. A rule of thumb: 2 watts per square foot *at least.* So if your kitchen is 20 by 20 (as mine is), that would mean 800 watts of electricity. I have over 1,000 watts operating (two pendants over the island, 100 watts each; a double pendant over the table, 200 more; three low halogens over the sink, 75 each; plus undercounter fluorescents; a surface-mounted fixture, 75 watts; and a total of five lamps). I went for extra power because my cabinets are dark ebony and the floor is deep terracotta, and both absorb light. Even with the extra wattage, the kitchen is not overly lit.

[TOP] A DOUBLE-HEIGHT CEILING CALLS FOR LOTS OF LIGHT. A SECONDARY ROW OF ANGLED WINDOW LETS IN THE SKY. WHEN THE SUN GOES DOWN, TRACK LIGHTING, HI-HATS, AND A PAIR OF CHANDELIERS ARE TURNED UP.

[ABOVE] IN THIS TIGHT SPOT, YOU WANT A LIGHT THAT DOESN'T GENERATE HEAT—THAT IS, A FLUORESCENT. CONCEALED BEHIND A LIGHT VALANCE OR A RECESSED CABINET BASE, FLUORESCENT BULBS ARE A SMART-LOOKING—AND AN ENVIRONMENTALLY FRIENDLY AND INEXPENSIVE—SOLUTION.

Recessed lights, which are sunk into the ceiling, can be helpful over a kitchen counter, too, especially in an area with no upper cabinets. They provide a headlight ray of light. The light does not spread or fill the space but directs a beam onto a target. If you are using recessed lights as task lighting, then the lights must be mounted directly above the surface you are working on. (Cautionary tale: One customer had a kitchen with plenty of recessed lights, yet none located directly over the counter itself. As she leaned over the cutting board one evening, her body came between the light source and the job at hand. She was slicing an onion and nicked her finger with the knife. Three stitches later, she was on the phone to her electrician.)

The recessed variety comes in a range of sizes, from 3 to 12 inches in diameter. Generally speaking, smaller is more chic and more discreet. Many recessed lights can be outfitted with a variety of bulb types, from pin spot to flood, narrow to wide, halogen to incandescent. They come in one of two voltages. You can opt for regular voltage and use incandescent bulbs, or go for the low voltage most often found in the smaller-aperture fixtures like my favorite, the MR 16. One caveat: While low-voltage bulbs use less electricity, they can interfere with other electronics, such as stereos and radios; even the lights themselves can hum. It's imperative that you have the light properly installed with the correct, specialized dimmer

FIELD NOTE

The hunger for light has been the driving force behind many a renovation project for Kristiina Ratia, who grew up in Finland. In the kitchen of her Connecticut farmhouse, she first replaced a pair of solid wood doors with a large pair of mullioned French doors. Several years later, she raised the roof to make the kitchen feel barn-like and added the unexpected and modern touch of wide and eye-filling skylights. Rather than ordering just the standard rectangular or square skylights, Kristiina had a local glass company custom-fabricate oversized skylights to maximize the skylit area in the unusual roofline of her soaring space. Running the skylights parallel to the multiplaned roof line (instead of just plunking a rectangle in the middle of the ceiling) meant the apertures could be made bigger to corral every bit of available light. Instantly, the room was inundated with sunlight. Eager for even more exposure, Kristiina had both a single-glass French door and a double-hung window installed on the wall leading to the porch. Now light pours in from virtually every angle.

TRADE TIP

If you mount your high hats (recessed ceiling fixtures) too close to the cabinet fronts, you will get a scalloped effect on the face of the cabinets. Instead, install recessed lights 12 to 15 inches off the front of your upper cabinets—even with the outer edge of the base cabinets.

[RIGHT] HI-HATS OF DIFFERENT DIMENSIONS (4 AND 8 INCHES), AN ANTIQUE BILLIARD LAMP, AND UNDER-COUNTER FLUORESCENTS (VERY GREEN OF US) CREATE LOVELY OVERALL ILLUMINATION.

(either electronic or magnetic) to cut down on all audible distractions.

Ambient lighting illuminates the room as a whole. This type of lighting is designed to guide you from point A to point B without your stumbling over the furniture or the dog. With this type of light, you're not aware of the source per se but rather the overall amount and quality of luminosity. Unlike the headlight-like directional beam of recessed lights, the ambient source emits a diffuse illumination. And while recessed lights are sunk into a ceiling, incognito-style, ambient lights are surface-mounted so you see the whole of the fixtures—making them decorative elements in and of themselves. Anything from milky glass vintage-style lights (like the type found in old school-houses) to elaborate chandeliers is an ambient candidate.

To ensure that the room is evenly lit, some designers plot a series of small fixtures in a grid pattern on the ceiling. Selective use of recessed fixtures can also amp up the overall lighting quotient and complement ambient light if you place them wisely: into the corners of the rooms and in front of glass windows and doors. What you want to avoid is positioning a down light (or any dramatic beam) so it shines on your face as you're sitting at the breakfast nook—

[ABOVE] A VERY MODERN TAKE ON A TRADITIONAL LIGHT: CLASSIC MILK-GLASS GLOBES, ALONG WITH TECH-Y TRACK SPOTS, HANG FROM A STAINLESS-STEEL TRACK.

[OPPOSITE] A WONDERFUL OLD OIL LAMP, COMPLETE WITH THE ORIGINAL SMOKE GUARDS, IS REBRASSED, RETROFITTED, AND REWIRED TO ILLUMINATE AN ISLAND. RECESSED LIGHTS FLANK THE PERIMETERS RAISING THE OVERALL LEVEL OF LIGHT.

TRADE TIP

What do you say to a naked bulb? Cover up! You have options to avoid having to stare into undercabinetry lighting, right at eye level. The most common and least stylish solution is provided by cabinetmakers: a light valance, or a 2-inch strip of woodwork that looks like an afterthought at best. Instead of accepting this solution, request that your cabinetmaker recess the interior cabinet base a bit (so the cabinet door extends beyond the bottom shelf). This simple detail will create an invisible light valance. Another trick: If you have an especially reflective countertop—polished granite or marble, for example—and the undercabinet lights give off glare, you can order a veiled lens from your local lighting dealer to pop over the offending bulbs.

none too flattering. No one wants to be scrutinized while standing directly under a recessed light—it's instantly aging.

Accent lighting directs your eye toward a specific spot in the room, whether a well-set table, a vase of flowers, or a child's work of art. This lighting takes the form of lamps on a counter, pendants over an island, or wall-mounted sconces. Accent lighting is also referred to as mood lighting because the light that's cast is warm and soft—as close to candlelight as you'll find in the artificial realm. I'm especially drawn to pendants—fixtures that are suspended, typically over an island or a table, and set an intimate tone. If you choose one with a translucent milk glass or a spear glass globe (as opposed to an opaque glass), you'll also increase the overall ambient light in the room. Any type of accent light can be put on a dimmer at any time, even after installation. For a minimal expense, a dimmer lets you adjust the lighting at the spin of a dial or tweak of a lever—from efficiently bright to romantically subdued.

Think of lighting fixtures as the jewelry of a room. They can be hip and hard-edged, extravagant, eccentric, or romantic. And there are countless resources and ways to track them down. Start with the basics: cata-

logues and home stores. You might also try Googling key words, like "alabaster fixture" or "iron lantern," and see where the search leads you. In terms of assessing quality on screen, I find that a well-designed website—whether an auction site, an online store, or a manufacturer's home page (which gives you a look at products and a list of store locations)—is often a good indication of well-made products. Often cities have lighting districts or design center buildings, where you can visit showroom upon showroom, all in one swoop.

[TOP] THERE'S NOTHING LIKE OLD-FASHIONED LAMP LIGHTING TO CREATE A SENSE OF SPACE. A SIMPLE PLUGGED-IN LIGHT AND VOILÀ—YOU'VE CREATED A BAR!

[ABOVE] BROWN ABSORBS 90 PERCENT OF AVAILABLE LIGHT. IF YOUR KITCHEN HAS DARK COLORS, ERR ON THE SIDE OF OVERLIGHTING. THESE BEAM-MOUNTED SPOTS DIRECT LIGHT ONTO THE COUNTER BELOW.

[OPPOSITE] THE SMALLER THE PENDANT, THE LOWER THE PLACEMENT. THE LARGER THE PENDANT, THE HIGHER THE PLACEMENT.

Don't overlook old fixtures you may already own. It is surprisingly easy to rewire and replate an old fixture, rendering it like new. Antique stores and fairs are another source of beautiful lights. What I love about vintage fixtures is that they're almost always one of a kind. Hanging alabaster bowls happen to be my favorite; a classic, they never lose their appeal or value. Of course, glass or crystal fixtures may not be easy to find in perfect condition, as they're fragile to begin with. Fixtures made of metal or wrought iron, on the other hand, are more prevalent in the antique market because they tend to hold up over time.

Lighting Lingo

Given that lighting is technical, it helps to understand what different types of fixtures and bulbs do. Here, the key terms defined and demystified.

Fluorescent.
This type of bulb generates a diffuse, shadowless light that's great under the counter (for tasks like chopping veggies) but tricky overhead. Too much of this bland, flat light has an unflattering effect, turning your kitchen into a K-Mart. On the bright side, fluorescents are cost-efficient—they last ten times longer than a regular lightbulb—and they're energy-efficient. If each of us changed just a couple of lightbulbs in our home to fluorescents, it would save the world a huge amount of energy. On the down side, these lights have an annoying tendency to hum. If you do opt for fluorescents, look for the models with an instant starter mechanism, which quiets the noise. While you're at it, look into the newer, warmer types.

Incandescent.
Mr. Edison's invention uses a continuous spectrum of color to form a soft white light in a range of wattage from 15 to 150. This warm, flattering light makes everything look like a day in the sun—which is why incandescents remain the first choice for lamps, pendants, sconces, and surface-mounted light fixtures. Unfortunately, the bulbs are inefficient; 90 percent of their effort goes into generating heat rather than illuminating. They have a short life, and they lose their luster as they age.

TRADE TIP

Deciding exactly where to locate a pendant, whether over a table, island, or countertop, can be tricky. First, aim for dead center over the space, knowing that if you happen to be off by an inch or so, no one will likely notice. As for height, pendants generally hang 30 to 34 inches above table height, 60 to 64 inches from the floor, and 66 to 72 inches off the floor above an island. Rules of thumb aside, nothing beats taking a look. Have someone hold up the fixture (or an object of comparable size) and see for yourself. Test-drive the height by viewing the light from its intended vantage point, whether sitting at the table or standing at the island.

Hi-Hats.
Also known as cans, pot lights, and down lights, hi-hats are recessed fixtures sunk into the ceiling that concentrate light downward. Avoid relying on just hi-hats for lighting your kitchen—you would need a shotgun's worth of them, and any more than eight or so can create the dreaded pockmarked ceiling effect. Be sure to choose the most unobtrusive trim piece, also known as a baffle, available.

Halogen.
Tiny halogen lights give off a bright, white light but also plenty of heat—enough to char a cabinet surface, which is why only low-voltage halogens are recommended for under-cabinet lighting. The low-voltage halogens and their cousins, the low-voltage xenons, are ideal for recessed lighting. These mighty little lights, which cost more than regular bulbs, don't need to be changed as often, and their small size makes them more inconspicuous in the ceiling. Caveats: Low-voltage halogens require

FIELD NOTE

Mixing moods and eras of lighting can work brilliantly. Take a cue from the iconoclastic scheme on full display in the dramatic East Hampton kitchen of Raymond Waites, a product designer in the home furnishings field, and his partner, Russell Berge. A pair of ornate, impossibly romantic, triple-tiered crystal chandeliers of Waites's own design dangle from the double-height ceiling over a billiard-table-size cooking island. But lest he do the expected, Waites also mounted track lighting on an industrial metal track spanning the room, allowing him to angle spots onto his ever-expanding and evolving collection of rare china pieces in a floor-to-ceiling display case.

As a designer, Waites certainly knows the rules, but he has the confidence to flout them. The combination of lighting fixtures is pure magic. With the kitchen's vaulted ceilings, working fireplace, and generous proportions, Waites could indulge his style of decorating *and* entertaining—all theater, with a great meal as the finale. When people are over, a candelabra is set atop the island and Waites, a great cook and a natural showman, performs for an admiring audience.

special dimmers to avoid annoying hums, and learning to replace the bulb, which has metal pins that must be clamped into the fixture, takes a little practice and patience.

Surface Mounts and Hanging Fixtures.

These lights are not recessed, and can take the form of a sleek dome dropping just 3 inches from the ceiling or an extravagant chandelier hanging 30 inches above counter height. As a bonus, surface-mounted fixtures, be they chandeliers, pendants, or lanterns, all use the same electrical junction box. You can specify one fixture now and change your mind later without having to redo the electrical work.

Track Lighting. With lighting heads that mount and move along an electrified track, track lighting is highly flexible. It's easy to add or subtract light sources. The individual lighting heads—tech-y halogen lights or mini pin dots—can be swiveled in any direction. Just be watchful of placement, lest an exposed lightbulb be angled directly into your eyes.

Illuminating an Electrical Plan

Smart lighting doesn't just appear out of the sky. You'll need a plan relatively early in the construction process. The plan should include designated locations for all appliances, audiovisual components, computers, and telephones—and, last but not least, any and all hardwired light sources, from pendants to recessed to under-the-counter. Think about the location of tabletop and standing lamps as well (called portables in the industry); they will need to be plugged into standard duplex outlets.

If you're not a lighting expert yourself—and how many of us are?—you're going to need help. Some people rely on the electrician, but his or her training is in wire management, not lighting design. Lighting is such a complex issue, and one with such tangible decorative and lifestyle implications, that it's wise to invest in real expert advice.

The most expert expert, of course, is a bona fide light-

[RIGHT] BRINGING THE OUTDOORS IN . . . HANDSOME EXTERIOR LANTERNS, COMPLETE WITH METAL SMOKE GUARDS, ARE RETROFITTED AND REWIRED TO ILLUMINATE AN ISLAND.

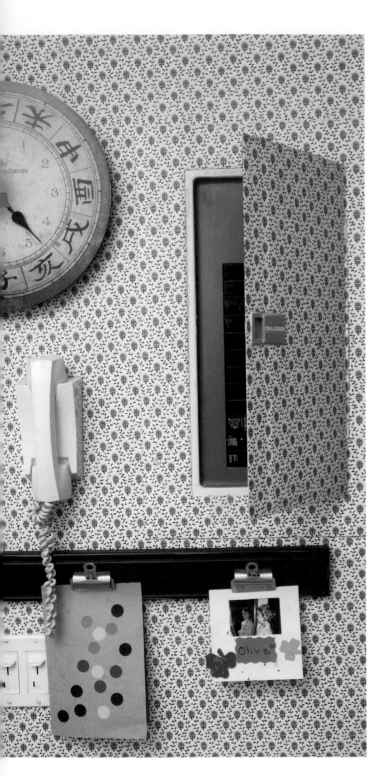

ing designer. He or she will add expense, both in terms of fee and, likely, in the quantity and brand of fixtures specified, but is most likely to deliver a sexy and seductive lighting plan. At the least, ask the architect or kitchen designer (and the electrician as well) to give you a scheme that denotes lighting placement to use as a jumping-off point.

Whoever you consult, get involved from the start. I recommend coming up with your own nascent plan and then bouncing it off the expert. Don't leave the details up to someone who doesn't know your family's needs and habits. Think the lighting through. Overthink it.

Start by playing "air-kitchen." Go through the motions of a normal day. Pantomime entering your home with your arms full of groceries, backpacks, a laptop, a dog on a leash, or a child or two. Where would you instinctively reach to switch on a light? Next, pile your belongings somewhere—where is that? The island, the desk, the counter next to the fridge? You'll need good overall light to unpack the groceries or sort the mail. Then do a dry run of cooking: Open the fridge to pull out ingredients– where will you place the food to be peeled and chopped? You'll need a task light there. Open your cabinets, upper and lower; you'll need to be able to see their contents. Where will you eat or set out a buffet? That's the spot for an accent light or two. Each slice of the kitchen needs to have the right light shed on it.

With these basic needs assessed, it's time to put your ideas on paper. As soon as you have in hand a working floor plan of the kitchen—generated by an architect, contractor, cabinetmaker, kitchen designer, or you yourself—get out the tracing paper and draw on top of it. Divide the room horizontally into lighting zones: low (lamps), middle (pendants and undercabinet), and upper (recessed and surface mounts).

With your tracing paper, lay out a pattern of lights (don't worry about specifying electrical locations for the appliances—just hand your electrician your floor plan and the appliance spec sheets, and the locations will be self-evident). Keep in mind that ceiling height also affects lighting design. High ceilings mean more lights, lower ceilings fewer. Try to balance the pattern; remember, symmetry is beauty, so don't cluster fixtures in one area, rendering the ceiling a raisin bread of Sheetrock. Occasionally, you may need to add a meaningless light simply to even out the overall pattern.

This is also the time to give thought to other electrical accessories—both for necessity (smoke, motion, and carbon monoxide detectors) and fun (stereo speakers and the like). It's also a good time to review your basic electrical system, to make sure it can handle the electrical load of your new appliances and lighting. You may need to upgrade an antiquated system.

Your plan may look crowded on paper, but remember that a ceiling represents a major portion of a room's total surface area. A logical layout will make the design seem deliberate rather than random, cohesive rather than chaotic.

Flipping the Switch

While you're putting energy into a lighting scheme, give some thought to the placement of the switches and outlets. I advocate a straightforward approach. You don't want to have to think twice or cross the room to flip on a light. Or two. As for grouping multiple switches, don't cluster too many or you'll be fumbling in the dark, trying to remember which switch goes to what spot—the island, the pantry, the garage. If do you end up ganging a couple together, put your most frequently used switch first at hand and the least-used switch farthest down the line. And if, for whatever reason, you need to gang more than four switches in a single location, separate the switching plates into two tiers.

While a switch is just a switch, a switch with a dimmer is something else altogether. For ambiance, variety, and sheer sense of control, dimmers are indispensable. They enable you to adjust the level of light to your liking, up and down and in between. With the exception of fluorescents, any type of light can be dimmed.

That said, not all dimmers are created equal—a simple lever type costs only a few dollars, while a sophisticated touch-tap system runs into the hundreds, even thousands. And while the sensitive touch-tap panels are smart, they can be too sensitive for some. Like me. I inevitably overtap these tap-style dimmers, shooting right past my desired light level. I prefer the simpler so-called DIVA (it's not)—a tiny slide button to the side of the actual switch that moves up and down easily and comes in at the bottom of the price spectrum.

As pedestrian as they are, outlets must be planned for as well. Again, think logistically.

Once you install an outlet, you don't want to incur the cost or the mess involved in moving it. For outlets slated to be installed on a backsplash, request that the electrician mount them close to the countertop rather than equidistant between counter and upper cabinet, as is the usual practice. Who wants to see the toaster cord snaking up to the outlet? For an island work surface, install the outlet on the least visible side of the island.

The goal is to have these utilitarian outlets, and their attendant switchplates, live unobtrusively in your kitchen. If your backsplash is a cocoa-colored marble, do you really want a white plastic switchplate glaring out like a Post-it note on the page? On the other hand, matching a colored plate cover to the surface often ends up looking forced. The best option is a metal switchplate in stainless steel, nickel, or oil-rubbed bronze, which makes for a quiet, sophisticated detail.

[ABOVE] KEEP THE BACKSPLASH AS CLEAR AND FREE OF ELECTRICAL INTERRUPTIONS AS POSSIBLE. REQUEST THAT OUTLETS BE POSITIONED LOW, NEAR THE COUNTERTOP, RATHER THAN SMACK IN THE CENTER OF THE SPLASH.

WISING UP ABOUT WIRES

It's hard to get turned on by electrical talk, but it will serve you well to educate yourself about simple electrical symbols—for both a current project or any renovation down the road.

ELECTRIC SYMBOLS

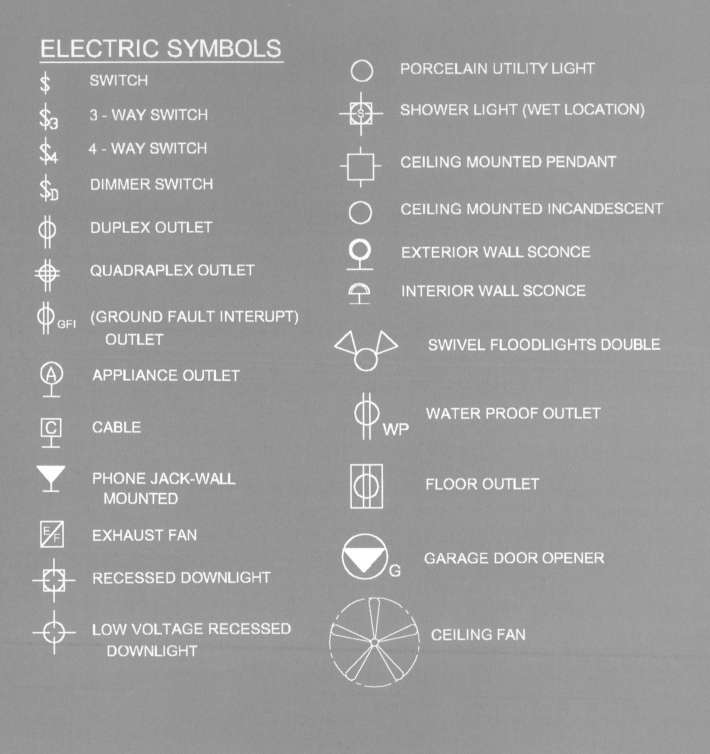

$	SWITCH
$3	3 - WAY SWITCH
$4	4 - WAY SWITCH
$D	DIMMER SWITCH
	DUPLEX OUTLET
	QUADRAPLEX OUTLET
GFI	(GROUND FAULT INTERUPT) OUTLET
A	APPLIANCE OUTLET
C	CABLE
	PHONE JACK-WALL MOUNTED
E/F	EXHAUST FAN
	RECESSED DOWNLIGHT
	LOW VOLTAGE RECESSED DOWNLIGHT

	PORCELAIN UTILITY LIGHT
S	SHOWER LIGHT (WET LOCATION)
	CEILING MOUNTED PENDANT
	CEILING MOUNTED INCANDESCENT
	EXTERIOR WALL SCONCE
	INTERIOR WALL SCONCE
	SWIVEL FLOODLIGHTS DOUBLE
WP	WATER PROOF OUTLET
	FLOOR OUTLET
G	GARAGE DOOR OPENER
	CEILING FAN

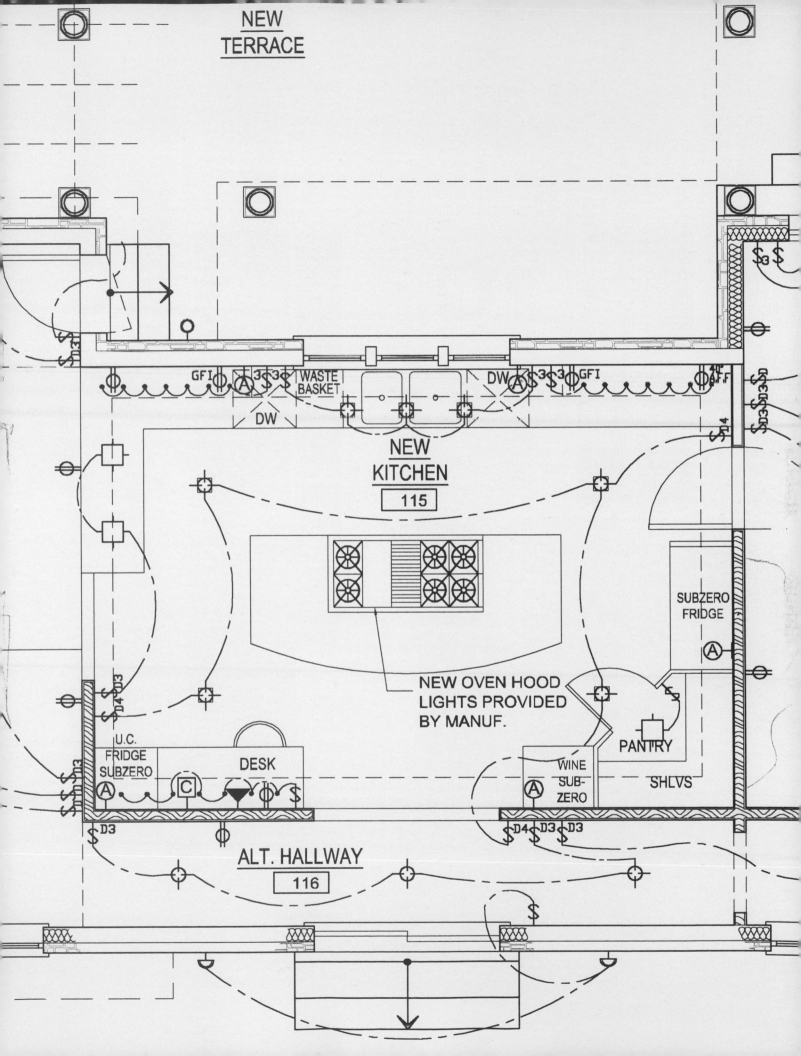

Auxiliary Spaces

Where do you put all the food that doesn't fit neatly into your regular cabinets—the boxes of pasta, cans of tomatoes, bottles of water or pinot noir? Where do you stack the extra dishes and stow the lobster pot? What about the paper towels and lightbulbs? And where do you kick off muddy boots or pile old magazines to toss out? If you're lucky, not in the thick of your primary kitchen space, which ideally should be kept clear for cooking and cleaning up, but rather in an auxiliary area.

While you may not be able to enlarge your kitchen proper without tremendous expense for knocking down load-bearing walls and relocating waste lines and water pipes, you may be able to find existing space to convert into an adjunct of the kitchen. In fact, pantries, mudrooms, and wine cellars are increasingly the most asked-for amenities on many a remodeler's or new homeowner's wish list. They help make the kitchen itself function smoothly. Small, smartly turned-out auxiliary spaces are prime real estate. So don't overlook them, like I did, when I was young and naïve. When my husband and I married, we had an apartment with an 8 by 10-foot windowless space next to the kitchen and directly across from the entry. We basically ignored it. Whenever my mother visited, she eyed it with envy, saying she'd give up a bedroom for that extra kitchen space. At that point in my life, with few dishes and no kids, I simply could not fathom what she meant. Now, thirty years later, I understand the value of such a small,

seemingly inconsequential spot. Adjunct spaces aren't the primary part of a plan, and sometimes they're an afterthought, but believe me, they're worth it. They allow all that extra paraphernalia for cooking, the lineup of empty recyclables, the bulk mail, the jumble of soccer cleats, to be tucked away but still close at hand.

The Pantry

There's no such thing as too much storage space. And a pantry, whether the size of a coat closet or a walk-in closet, remains the best solution for handling kitchen overflow. Before the era of modern appliances and refrigeration, kitchens were reserved for cooking. A room with a hearth, the kitchen was bordered by other spaces meant for purely storage purposes: larders, cold storage rooms, and pantries (basically, multiple closets with open shelves used to store foodstuffs, cleaning supplies, dishes, and china). In the 1980s, kitchen design often incorporated the pantry as a compact cabinet loaded

[OPPOSITE] THE ULTIMATE MUD-ROOM. WITH WAINSCOTED WALLS, LARGE WOOD CUBBIES, A BUREAU, AND A BENCH, THIS ROOM MAKES A GREAT FIRST—AND LAST—IMPRESSION.

[ABOVE] THIS PANTRY WORKS AS WELL TODAY AS IT DID MORE THAN A HUNDRED YEARS AGO WHEN IT WAS FIRST CONSTRUCTED, COMPLETE WITH GLASS-DOORED CABINETS, BIN LATCHES, STAINLESS-STEEL COUNTERTOP AND SINK, AND A HARDWOOD FLOOR. WHERE THIS PANTRY ONCE STORED FINE CHINA AND SUPPLIED A BUTLERED DINING ROOM, IT NOW SERVES AS A RECYCLING CENTER AND AN AD HOC STORAGE AREA.

[OPPOSITE] THIS PANTRY WITH ELEGANT ETCHED GLASS DOORS ACCOMMODATES STORAGE OVERFLOW—FROM FOOD TO PAPER GOODS TO LARGE PARTY PLATTERS.

with too-shallow shelves and swing-out amenities that were more awkward than useful. Now we are returning to the pantry as it was originally—surprise, surprise—conceived: a room unto itself in which you can stow kitchen clutter efficiently out of sight and out of the way.

Utilitarian in purpose as it is, though, a pantry needn't be a dark little stuffy room crammed with cans and boxes. You can turn out a pantry with plenty of style. Wainscot walls give the interior warmth and charm, for example. Or you could paint the walls and shelves a handsome color in a durable, enamel paint. If you think creatively, a pantry can even have personality. I had a client who decided, at the suggestion of her daughter, to line a wall of the pantry with a custom-made bulletin board. While Mom stocks the shelves, the daughter tacks up artwork and school schedules.

A pantry can also benefit the look of the kitchen itself by liberating it from excessive cabinetry. By consolidating a lot of stuff into an out-of-sight room, you may gain more light and

airiness in the kitchen proper. Having less cabinetry may actually allow you to keep or add windows over a counter, or doors to the outside, offering natural light. A pantry can ease the budget as well. With its simple construction, often built on site, and floor-to-ceiling shelving, a pantry is usually far less expensive than a new bank of custom cabinets.

The time to determine where to fit a new pantry into your plan, or how to retrofit an existing space, is when you're planning the overall kitchen layout. Size up your kitchen, all the dead spaces and corners, as well as all the perimeter nooks and hallways and the adjacent rooms. Can you steal space from the nearby laundry room? Can you flank the fridge with shelving covered by glass doors to create the look of a nook? One thing to remember: The pantry should be located in a cool spot, not in the path of direct sunlight or backed up to a wall with a southern exposure, or food will have a shorter shelf life!

If you're working with an old pantry, there's a good chance you'll want to redesign it. Many pantries designed more than twenty years ago tend to be small and highly compartmentalized. My kitchen came with a pantry like that, and it didn't work for my family. It consisted of built-in cabinets and lots of cutlery drawers, more like an old-fashioned butler's pantry, which served the dining room by holding china, crystal, and flatware. While such storage is nice to have near the dining room, what I needed, and what many of my clients need, is a pantry space in, or just off, the kitchen, with open shelves to store not only canisters of flour and sugar but also big items like bags of dog kibble, flats of juice boxes, and multiple jars of peanut butter and tomato sauce.

A pantry is all about shelving. You'll determine the length and depth of the shelves as well as their configuration (*U*-shaped, *L*-shaped, or a single wall's worth) based on the dimensions of the space. Think about how much floor space you want to leave free for newspaper recycling, backpacks, pet food. You also want to think about standing in the space. If it's too cramped because it's so crammed with shelves, you'll find yourself with your arms at your sides and no room to turn around. The extra shelving may not be worth cutting into the comfort zone.

As for shelf depth, figure you need at least 12 inches to accommodate a single row of cereal boxes. Fifteen inches allows for multiple rows of canned goods or stacks of bowls, dishes, and platters. You can also consider a combination of shelf depths—deeper on the back wall, shallower on the side—or a gradated, incremental plan, with the deepest shelves on the bottom for heavier items and shallower in the upper regions, which can make the space feel less claustrophobic. Word of advice: Don't go too deep. Anything over 18 inches and food items disappear into a storage abyss.

The distance between shelves matters, too. Not all spacing is equal. Don't feel obligated to position the shelves evenly apart. By varying the height between them, you can accommodate a range of foods or appliances. Most important, don't take the shelving all the way down to the floor. It's a good idea to leave enough height under the bottommost shelf for tall, heavy things like bags of charcoal and flats of bottled water. You don't want to have to lift them onto a shelf—even a shelf

TRADE TIP

If you're lucky enough to have a pantry space wider than 6 feet, consider putting it to more use than just food storage. With 24-inch-deep cabinetry on one side and 18-inch shelving on the other, you still have plenty of space in the back for a secondary appliance—an extra dishwasher, a potting sink, or a small wine fridge.

[ABOVE] TEAK COUNTERTOPS DIFFERENTIATE THE PANTRY FROM THE NEIGHBORING KITCHEN. MORE THAN JUST A DESIGN ELEMENT, THE TEAK IS SOFTER AND LESS LIKELY TO CHIP FINE CHINA AND CRYSTAL.

FIELD NOTE

The Fullers of Rye, New York, a large, blended family of cooks and entertainers, had designed their dream kitchen but were stuck on one issue. They happened to have incomparable water views on both sides of the kitchen, which would be sacrificed by cabinets if they were to accommodate their storage needs. Storage versus sunlight and view. What to do?

Their former home had a capacious pantry, and the Fullers were determined to replicate such an adjunct space in their new kitchen. They found the spot, sandwiched between the Sub-Zero refrigerator and the wine cooler. To make the pantry accessible in the crowded corner, they placed the door on the diagonal, making use of what would have been dead space. The new pantry, albeit not quite as large as their previous one, provides floor-to-ceiling storage on two walls. Every day they look out at the water, they're grateful they chose to keep the view free and clear.

Menu
WILSON BRAND
HIGH GRADE
CATSUP
OCTOBER
HAPPY KIDS
PEANUT BUTTER

CARROTS
BREAD
EGGS
RICE
CHEESE

just a few inches off the floor surface. Shelves should be most tightly spaced in the prime storage area—arm and eye level—saving the tallest regions for the most seldom used items, whether party-size salad bowls or tall vases. Any shelf higher than 7 feet is inaccessible even with a footstool.

Most kitchens are well served by one main pantry, but I've had clients with spacious enough homes who've asked for an additional one or two rooms for other types of storage. While the main pantry holds foodstuffs, another could house platters, dishes, and oversized serving pieces, and a third might accommodate and organize school and art supplies or act as a broom closet for the vacuum, mop, and stepstool.

Then there's the question of whether or not to close off the pantry with a door. A door may not be necessary if the straight-on view of the interior is attractive: plates neatly stacked, teacups hung from hooks, all the foodstuffs stored on the side shelves. Most people want to be able to shut the door on all that kitchen content, however, especially if the pantry is in a well-trafficked area or the kitchen proper.

Shutting off the pantry can be as simple as hanging a door that's in the same design vocabulary as the neighboring household doors or nearby kitchen cabinetwork. That way, the pantry doesn't stand out but rather melds into the overall look of the house. Alternatively, you could make a real style statement with the door. Etched glass is quite pretty, and the etching itself artfully obscures the view inside. If you go with a plain glass door, you can always partially curtain it, in the French mode. A pantry door can also be a personal canvas. One client of mine took the molding from around her old pantry, complete with her four kids' handwritten growth

[LEFT] CARPENTRY (BUILT ON SITE BY A LOCAL CARPENTER) RATHER THAN CABINETRY (FABRICATED AT A CABINET FACTORY) WORKS BEST FOR A WALK-IN PANTRY LIKE THIS.

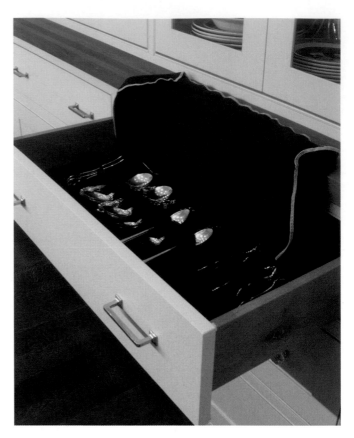

[ABOVE LEFT] SOME THINGS YOU JUST HAVE TO TAKE WITH YOU, AND THIS WALL CHART (CHRONICLING FOUR KIDS' GROWTH) WAS ONE OF THEM. THE FAMILY REMOVED THE MOLDING FROM THEIR FORMER HOME AND HAD IT REINSTALLED AROUND THE FRAME OF THEIR NEW BROOM CLOSET.

[ABOVE RIGHT] CUTLERY DRAWERS LINED WITH PACIFIC CLOTH (THE ANTITARNISH FABRIC VISIBLE HERE) MAKE USING THE GOOD SILVER MUCH EASIER.

TRADE TIP

If you have a single closet but need it to serve several functions, think about subdividing it with a partial or full Sheetrock wall. For example, you'll want to separate sportswear and gear from coats. (Who wants the smell of damp sweat to permeate your cashmere pea coat?) Ditto with pet supplies or cleansers with strong chemical odors.

charts, and remounted it framing the pantry door in her new home. This way, they kept a little of their family history intact.

Remember that if you opt for a door and you like to keep it closed, you're going to need a free hand to reach for the knob. One way around that: a swinging door (or two). That's what I decided to do in my own pantry. For me, the swinging door (which has no handles) means I don't have to put down bags of groceries outside the pantry; I can walk right in. And I made sure the doors are free to swing wider than the conventional door swing of 90 degrees. The 180-degree hinges allow me to push through. More hidden benefits: The doors are never open, and they automatically swing shut behind me.

If in studying and reworking your kitchen plan you conclude there's simply no room for a bona fide pantry and you don't want to give up cabinet space for food storage, don't despair; think creatively. You can concoct a pseudo pantry by retrofitting a hutch or even carving out storage under the back stairs. Resist the temptation to install cabinet pantries in which the cabinet is fitted with swing-out or slide-out compartments. They tend to be expensive, cumbersome, and suited solely for stocking canned goods (not the way most of us shop today). Look for a space where you can throw open the doors and take stock of everything at a glance.

FIELD NOTE

The mudroom of the Chang-Scanlan house in Greenwich, Connecticut, is an object lesson in outfitting the buffer zone between inside and out. The family chose to wrap the room halfway up with wainscoting, which provides decorative interest as well as protection against bangs and scuffs. Next, for the floor, they installed stones of various sizes in shades of dusty brown to mask dirt—a real priority for the family. Between two active kids and a father who's a passionate organic gardener, sod and mud are constant invaders.

Pine furniture—including a large bench for sitting and untying shoes or parking groceries and an antique chest for scarf and shawl storage—creates the feeling of an actual room, not just a passageway. (Pine is a good choice for mudrooms because it's hardy—it can stand up to use and abuse.) As for other storage, the Chang-Scanlans chose to build tall, spacious cubbies. Each family member got his or her own 2-foot-wide closet, hung with hooks and personalized with a small landscape painting (done by a local artist) depicting that person's particular hobby. Beneath the cubbies went two shelves for shoes. The lower one is open to the floor so you can shove boots underneath or slide in-line skates in and out; the upper shoe shelf is reserved for dressier shoes you don't want to get scuffed. The family also had upper shelving built for oversized baskets—great for storing mittens, hats, and scarves. Closed closets, at the edge of the mudroom, finish off this perfectly sized and perfectly designed space.

WINE CELLARS

For most wine drinkers who like to keep a few bottles or a case or two at hand, a refrigerator or under-counter wine cooler suffices. For others—oenophiles or serious collectors—nothing but a bona fide wine cabinet or cellar will do. In that case, you have to step out of the kitchen to look at your options. It would be nice if you could simply appropriate unused space near the kitchen—under the back stairs or in an adjacent garage, perhaps. The truth is that wine needs a certain environment (climate and humidity) to stay drinkable and valuable. Overheating ages the grape prematurely, and excessive light can turn a good bottle bad. That's why wines belong in wine *cellars*—that is, in the basement, where the air is always cooler and there's little light. In addition, the lowest floor in the house is the most stable, so racks are unlikely to rattle (no wonder we retreat to the basement in a hurricane). Stability is almost as critical to grape storage as temperature. Once you've decided to go south, you need to figure out the scope of your interest—and the size of your investment.

The first choice is a wine cabinet, which sounds small but can actually hold anywhere from a few dozen to a few hundred bottles. This freestanding piece of furniture is a serious work of carpentry and cooling; it has to be, in order to support a cooling system as well as the weight of the bottles themselves (each bottle weighs about 3 pounds; multiply that by a few hundred, and you're talking a substantial load). Don't skimp on the quality of the construction or the cabinet can torque over time, putting your collection at risk.

For a full-fledged wine cellar, you'll need to carve out an actual room that can be sealed off with a door and finished properly so that it's waterproof and insulated. Allow room for enough racks, either modular or custom, made of sturdy pine or redwood. (Allow roughly 1 linear foot of wall for every 125 bottles of wine.) If the wine room has fluctuations of temperature, you'll need to consult an HVAC contractor about installing a dedicated air-conditioning zone. Lighting is key; make sure the bulbs have a thermal-fused lens so the fixtures don't give off too much heat. Floor choices for optimum cooling range from concrete to slate or even marble. Other details, such as French doors or a tasting table, give a wine cellar style. After all, anyone with a wine cellar is going to want to show it off!

The Kitchen Office: A Room Within a Room

Once upon a time, a kitchen office was not much more than a nook for cookbooks and perhaps a bulletin board. But now, bigger kitchens, more time spent in those kitchens (doing things other than cooking), and more mobile technology have created the need for full-fledged mini offices.

After all, the kitchen is where we organize the bulk of our household activities, peruse the kids' schedules, plan the family's meals, make phone calls to pediatricians and coaches, check e-mails. A dedicated office area keeps the blitz of incoming papers off the island or countertops. Sounds like a tall order to accommodate this much business, but truthfully, you don't need much more than a bookshelf or two over a desk (or, as I call it, a desklet). Ideally, you'll want to locate the space close to a window and far from the stove or range, where cooking splatters can gunk up a computer keyboard. My advice is to allow a minimum of 30 linear inches for a surface, though 36 to 42 is even better. Frankly, any more than that and you will create too much of a real office feel—detracting from a kitchen's primary purpose and charm and inadvertently inviting more clutter. As for the desk itself, whether it's freestanding or built of coordinating cabinetry and anchored to the wall, it should be sturdy in order to support your office tech: computer, fax machine, phone, and whatever other electronic devices you access daily.

Wiring is the key to a well-connected kitchen. A combination telephone/Ethernet port (120-volt power outlet with surge protector) is essential to prevent overloading. While you're at it, have the electrician put in an outlet for plugging in a cell phone or digital camera charger as well as a separate circuit for the computer so it's protected from crashes due to the pull of electricity from the major appliances in the room. And don't forget lighting, either, since you'll be working at the desk with and without natural light. If you have a bookshelf above, I recommend incorporating a valance or undercabinet lights into the piece. Otherwise, you'll have to make room on the desk for

[ABOVE] AN OPEN PASS-THROUGH WINDOW KEEPS THIS KITCHEN COUNTER DESK FROM FEELING CLAUSTROPHOBIC. THE VIEW OF THE GREAT BEYOND ADDS IMMEASURABLY.

[OPPOSITE] I CALL THEM "DESKLETS." MY CUSTOMERS TELL ME THEY LIKE THEM COUNTER HEIGHT (36 INCHES) AND NOT TABLE HEIGHT (29 INCHES) FOR EASIER ACCESS. WHO HAS TIME TO ACTUALLY SIT DOWN IN THE KITCHEN? AT A COUNTER YOU CAN JUST PERCH!

a tabletop lamp, which can look great, but takes up valuable space. I can't tell you how often I have been asked to add undershelving lights after the fact. Keep in mind, this is not the time or place for low-voltage—that is, hot—bulbs. In a tight spot, especially one topped by an upper cabinet or bookcase, the last thing you want is to generate more heat. Incandescent or fluorescent bulbs are better options.

Outfitting the desk area with a few office accessories can help the whole family stay organized. Along with a bulletin board–cum–message center–cum-photo display, consider at least one file drawer and a pencil drawer or two (also known as a clutter catcher). As for mail sorting, forget diminutive cubbies or letter slots, which fill up too quickly. Instead, opt for a deep drawer or basket, preferably two: one for new mail, the other for mail to be answered.

Mudrooms

Mudrooms are the great buffer between the outside and the inside; they keep detritus from creeping into the kitchen and keep clutter and muck out. A mudroom is a place to unload gear, remove boots and dirty shoes, and hang coats and hats, so the kitchen is free to be a kitchen.

Mudrooms can range in size from barely bigger than a hall closet to almost as large as a bedroom. If you're starting from scratch, ideally you want a minimum of roughly 8 by 10 feet. A room that size allows for a 2-foot-deep closet along one wall and an 18-inch-deep storage unit—cubbies, shelving, or hooks—on the other. And you'll still have a generous 42-inch aisle in the center.

The best mudroom combines open and closed storage: a closet (where grown-ups can put their coats) along with sturdy hooks (for kids' wear, casual jackets, and dog leashes); open shelves for sweatshirts and scarves; and baskets or bins for sports equipment (remember, balls roll and hockey sticks teeter if left uncorralled).

As for cubbies, there was a time I used them constantly, and they became a trademark of sorts in the mudrooms I designed. The attraction, of course, is that they compartmentalize clutter, plus it's fun for each family member (or at least the kids) to have their own nook. What I've learned, from feedback over the years, is that cubbies create visual clutter; you can't close them off, so if

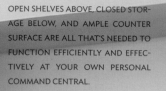

OPEN SHELVES ABOVE, CLOSED STORAGE BELOW, AND AMPLE COUNTER SURFACE ARE ALL THAT'S NEEDED TO FUNCTION EFFICIENTLY AND EFFECTIVELY AT YOUR OWN PERSONAL COMMAND CENTRAL.

[ABOVE] WATERPROOF BRICKS AND STONES MAKE A WONDERFUL SURFACE FOR A KITCHEN FLOOR. THIS WORN TERRA-COTTA SIMPLY ACQUIRES MORE PATINA AS DIRT AND DETRITUS ARE DEPOSITED ON ENTRY.

[LEFT] CUBBIES ARE GREAT, BUT NOTHING BEATS A ROW OF STURDY HOOKS WITH A WORN BENCH BELOW FOR A QUICK STOP AND DROP. FOR HEAVY-DUTY HANGING, BE SURE YOUR HOOKS ARE EITHER TETHERED TO A STUD OR MOUNTED ON A BOARD.

you have a sloppy kid, the cubby might always be messy. Then again, you may end up with blank squares when one or more kids leave the house. Parents may find themselves always arranging the contents—shifting them from cubby A to cubby B to look neat and maximize storage. An alternative to the cubby format is a wood board with sturdy oversized hooks and an attached open shelf or two above. A chamfered, or angled-in, decorative edge gives the shelf a finished look.

When considering how your mudroom will function, think about what you want to keep out of the kitchen. If there's enough space in the mudroom, you can locate all the recycling bins for papers and bottles there. A bench makes it easier for the kids to take off their soccer cleats, Rollerblades, or dirt-laden sneakers before tracking and trekking the stuff all over your carpet. A bench also provides a surface on which the kids can set their stuff while they are (you hope) putting the coats and cleats away. If you have pets, you can place a kitty litter box or a dog bed in a mudroom, keeping odors and dog hair out of the environment in which you cook and eat.

In an especially large mudroom space, a gardener might even have the luxury of hooking up a potting sink,

which means no more dragging branches of bittersweet in or dropping orange berries on the freshly mopped kitchen floor. For others of us, a second sink holds the promise of keeping dog baths and sneaker-scrubbing away from the kitchen sink. If you have a family of hikers and horseback riders, you might even consider having a floor drain put into the mudroom floor, as a friend of mine did. She simply pours a bucket of water over the floor when it's really mucky, and all the dirt disappears down the drain.

Some clients have requested a small stackable washer-dryer in the mudroom, and this notion makes sense on the face of it—kids can just shove the dirty uniforms in the washer when they come in. But if the mudroom is the primary entrance and family and friends are trekking past, the last thing you want on view is the laundry. If you can, keep the machines in a laundry room proper; if not, at least block them off with a door or a curtain.

While a mudroom is a catchall spot, it needn't be chaotic or messy or devoid of style. It should be a charming room, especially if it's the first space most family members and friends enter, and a smooth transition, stylistically, into the kitchen proper. Here's what to consider from the floor up. First, be sure your mudroom has a sturdy surface underfoot, one that does not show soil or dirt. This is one of the few times in a renovation when wood is not a great option. Wood tends to scratch and scar under an onslaught of sports shoes and warp from the wetness of rain and snow. Stone, on the other hand, is ideal for such a spot. Consider quartzite, slate, or tumbled marble—all are durable and come in earthy hues that help mask mud. Be sure to layer on a mat

[TOP] SOMETIMES THE SIMPLEST SOLUTION YIELDS THE MOST ELEGANT END PRODUCT. WHITE-PAINTED BEAD BOARD—EITHER THE ORIGINAL, INSTALLED BOARD BY BOARD, OR PURCHASED IN 4 BY 8-FOOT PANELS—IS A TIMELESS CLASSIC.

[ABOVE AND OPPOSITE] THE ORIGINAL, PRECUBBY VERSION OF A FAMILY-ONLY MUDROOM. PARK YOUR COATS AND BOOTS BEFORE YOU ENTER.

or a small sturdy rug at the entrance to the room for wiping feet.

Next up, the walls. Many renovators take the opportunity to install wainscoting because it not only makes the room feel finished (less like a walk-through closet) but also it's far more durable than a Sheetrock wall. Painted in a durable semigloss enamel, it's easy to wipe clean. Wallpaper is another way to go. It can add a splash of style in a fresh, cheerful stripe or a retro floral, and if it's vinyl-finished, it's also wipable. To add variety and charm to a wall that has space after you've put in a row of coat hooks, you can always consider hanging a framed poster or a kid's painting. If you want to be practical, consider an oversized bulletin board to supplement or even supplant a kitchen one. A big-enough board lets you pin up shopping lists, school notices, notes to each other, and

IF YOU CAN'T CLOSE THE DOOR TO THE LAUNDRY ROOM, AT LEAST TUCK THE APPLIANCES OUT OF SIGHT BEHIND A SHEETROCK "WING WALL."

IF THE LAUNDRY AREA IS BIG
ENOUGH, WHY NOT ADD
AMENITIES LIKE A TV OR A DVD
PLAYER TO EASE THE TEDIUM
OF IRONING SHIRTS?

holiday cards. The bulletin board can actually be a nice way to link the mudroom and the kitchen aesthetically, too, if you construct the bulletin board from the same molding as your cabinetry. Order a dozen extra feet of molding from the cabinet manufacturer and have a carpenter assemble the frame with a piece of cork surrounded by this custom detailing.

Laundry Rooms

No one wants a washer and dryer running all day long, smack in the middle of the kitchen. The basket of dirty clothes is none too appetizing, and the noise is distracting (it's one thing to hear the quiet hum of a dishwasher, another to endure the sloshing and whirring of the laundry machines).

When you have no choice (often the case in a city apartment), your goal should be to segregate the laundry in some fashion from the cooking and eating areas. One couple in Manhattan used a two-tiered peninsula to separate their stackable unit from the working kitchen. Hinged screens or curtains are other solutions.

On the subject of stackables, units come as small as 24 inches wide by 27 inches deep—that's pretty mini, and suitable for a single person or a family that doesn't have endless loads. No matter the dimensions, be sure to allow plenty of ventilation around the machines; overheated electrical appliances are the largest cause of fires in the United States! If you're going to close off your laundry facility behind a wall and door, consider using a shuttered or slat-vented one to allow air circulation around the machines. Extra wall insulation in the surrounding walls will cut down on

TRADE TIP

I'm hooked on the idea of hooks in a house, and the laundry room is no exception. Hooks can hold an array of items that would otherwise clutter a drawer or trip up on the floor: extension cords, mops and brooms, stuffed-to-the-max laundry bags, and the like. I prefer hooks to pegs, since things tend to slide off pegs. Look for hooks that are big and sturdy—at least 6 inches long—and anchored directly into a wall stud to secure your heaviest paraphernalia.

the noise factor, but this is only an option if you're building from scratch, since it's awkward and costly to add after the fact.

Instead of a stackable unit, you can opt for bigger-capacity side-by-side appliances that fit under a counter—in which case they must be front-loading. You need to allow 54 linear inches for these machines, which really means 66 inches to ensure proper ventilation. That's a big bite out of the kitchen's space.

Of course, none of these in-kitchen options allows for all the surrounding laundry stuff: clothes baskets, storage for detergents and bleaches, an iron, not to mention an ironing board or a soaking sink. If you have the choice, laundry should get its own dedicated space. Wherever you decide to design the room, try to locate it close to where the most laundry is generated: either near the back door or on the second floor, central to the bedrooms (make sure to install a leakproof pan underneath the washer so any overflow doesn't seep through the ceiling below).

The best laundry room is large enough to accommodate all your basic needs (what's better than an ironing board that's always up and ready?), and you should outfit it so that it can multitask. If the room is adjacent to the kitchen and the back door, for instance, think about installing a sink that's deep enough to work as a gardening sink. No matter where you locate the laundry room, try to incorporate a table in it that you and others can use as a sewing center or crafts area.

With a laundry room that offers this many activities, you may find yourself spending quite a bit of time in there, in which case I recommend hooking up a cable outlet for a little TV diversion. When I am stuck ironing seemingly countless collared shirts for my sons, I like to be able to catch a news update. I have a friend who keeps her fax machine in the laundry room. Her logic is that the fax is noisy and so is the washing machine, so why not pair them up? As a bonus, she says, her incoming faxes always smell fresh!

[RIGHT] THIS GENEROUS MUDROOM/LAUNDRY ROOM COMBO RECYCLED THE KITCHEN CABINETS FROM THE PREVIOUS RENOVATION. WHY NOT? IT USED TO BE THE KITCHEN.

The laundry room décor starts with the floor, which should be practical: washable and water-resistant. From a comfort standpoint, the floor should be cushiony to absorb any rattling from the washer and dryer. One of the best choices is also one of the most affordable: linoleum, available as sheets or tiles in a variety of colors (so you can checkerboard them for extra charm). You can also throw down a washable rug that's inexpensive enough to ditch and replace when it gets dingy. Even the machines can add a splash of style if you pick a bright color (blue or orange) or a sleek silver.

[ABOVE] IT'S NEVER TOO EARLY TO TEACH THEM THE ART OF DISPLAY—START BY DISPLAYING THEIR ART!

[LEFT] PACKING A LOT OF STYLE INTO A VERY SMALL MUDROOM: A CHECKER-BOARD FLOOR IN A CRAZY COLLAGE OF COLORS SETS A PLAYFUL TONE. AN ANTIQUE FRENCH STOVE GETS A NEW LIFE AS A STORAGE SPOT FOR MITTENS AND HATS.

[OPPOSITE] OFTEN RESERVED FOR USE AS A POWDER ROOM, THE SPACE UNDER THE STAIRS WORKS EQUALLY AS WELL AS A CENTRALLY LOCATED SPOT FOR THE LAUNDRY.

Survival Guide

It's hard to survive any renovation or construction, whether you're living through it amid all the plaster dust or designing from a safe distance. But a kitchen project takes the cake. When you think of all that a finished kitchen contains—refrigeration and flames, wiring and masonry, furniture and light fixtures—it's no wonder creating one, let alone the ideal one, is daunting.

The scary stories reverberate in the carpool line and at cocktail parties—tales of contractors who disappear, tile workers who leave the floor half finished, the plumber who cracks the counter while installing the faucet. But while a few hiccups are inevitable, if you follow basic guidelines and do a little homework, you can sidestep most disasters and come out of the process sane and happy.

Set a Budget and a Borrowing Strategy

A new kitchen can run anywhere from a few thousand dollars (the cost of laminate counters and a stainless-steel fridge) to a few hundred thousand dollars (a total makeover with the latest technological bells and whistles). You need to establish your spending limit—that is, the magic number you absolutely cannot go over in terms of dollars . . . and sense. At the same time, think big. This may sound contradictory, but don't throw in the dish towel on your dream of an eat-in kitchen with an island or that pro-style cooktop and wine chiller. There's always the option of borrowing. Look into home equity loans, which typically have low interest rates. If your house has appreciated since you purchased it (a bank-approved appraisal will establish the value), the equity may pay for your new kitchen. There are two basic kinds of home equity loans: lump sum—one check in one fell swoop—and line of credit. Opt for the latter, which you can draw upon as needed to pay for the project as it proceeds.

When calculating how much to spend on a renovation, remember that a kitchen investment may be worth the expense strictly from a resale point of view—what's called *recouped value*. According to the National Home Builders Association, you can expect to recapture 100 percent, or even more, of your kitchen remodeling costs, provided you don't turn out a kitchen that's so idiosyncratic (chartreuse cabinets and cherry-red appliances) that it turns off potential buyers. Keep in mind, too, that the newer the kitchen is, the better it shows and

the more chance it will help the sale of the house. But don't sink more money into a project than makes sense. Real estate experts advise not to spend more than 10 to 15 percent of the total value of your home on kitchen construction. Although this kind of resale advice is helpful, use your judgment when it comes to figuring out the equation. A $3 million house (if you're fortunate enough to own one) doesn't necessarily warrant a $450,000 kitchen!

Gather Your Forces

Behind every good kitchen project is a good team: the designer, contractor, plumber, electrician, lighting expert, stone or tile installer, and all the other tradespeople who come on board during a renovation. You'll be responsible for hiring at least one or two of the experts yourself: the architect (who may bring his or her own contractor along) and/or the general contractor (GC), who typically pulls together the rest of the team (subcontractors, or "subs").

Many people question whether they even need an architect, or if they can simply work directly with the GC. If the project is significant in scope and you're relatively short on experience, I'd vote for hiring an architect (or a designer with kitchen credentials) to help translate your goals and needs into an actual paper rendering. Most people and projects benefit by spending the money on these experts. They may even save money in the long run, sparing the expense of ripping out and redoing mistakes—from the placement of an outlet to the height of the backsplash. Architects are especially valuable if the project looks like it will involve variances, permits, engineers' reports, and land surveys, not to mention making a presentation to a historical society, if needed. While GCs and interior designers may be familiar with such issues, architects usually have more expertise in dealing with the technicalities as well as the personnel involved in gaining approvals.

Veteran renovators are a different story; they may have amassed enough knowledge to be confident in their own ability to design, even draw their ideas, themselves, and to work directly with the contractor. Some may even go so far as to act as the GC themselves—certainly a moneysaving proposition, but think it through. Chasing down tradespeople and keeping track of schedules and deliveries is time-consuming and headache-inducing.

Whether you hire an architect or deal directly with the GC, make sure you meet the person who will actually be on the job. You may interview the head of a firm only to discover that he or she is not the one you'll be working with day in and day out. Renovation and building require a rather intimate, if short-term, relationship with designers and construction workers. They're going to see you in your pajamas, hear your phone conversations, witness family squabbles . . . If you're not comfortable with them from the beginning, keep looking.

The following should go without saying, but I'll say it anyway. *Check references.* Homeowners know they're supposed to do their homework, but (familiar story) they find reasons not to! Hiring an architect or a contractor, like hiring a nanny, is part instinct, part research. Take ten minutes to make a few calls. Start with the Better Business Bureau. Hey, it's only one call; you can even check someone out online (www.bbb.org). As for personal references, ideally, you should talk to at least three. Most important is the last job the professional completed—that's the best example and predictor of that contractor's work. Ask the owner if it's possible to see the kitchen in person. There's no better recommendation than your own eyes.

When calling for a reference, keep a checklist nearby so you don't forget to ask key questions, such as:

[OPPOSITE] A SUCCESSFUL RENOVA-TION LIKE THIS ONE REQUIRES A PROJECT MANAGER AND A LOT OF TEAM PLAYERS. SOMEONE HAS TO BE RESPONSIBLE FOR ENSURING THAT ALL IS DONE CORRECTLY.

[ABOVE] CONSTRUCTION ETIQUETTE EXTENDS FAR BEYOND YOUR FRONT DOOR. YOUR RENOVATION WILL IMPACT YOUR NEIGHBORS. TO BE A WELL-MANNERED RENOVATOR, EN-SURE THAT STREET PARKING, DUMP-STER SITES, AND SANITATION ARE ALL AS MINIMALLY INVASIVE AS POSSIBLE.

- Was the job finished in the time promised?

- Did the job stay realistically within the budget, or did the designer or contractor woefully underestimate costs?

- Were there a lot of changes of details—what the industry calls *change orders*—during the process?

- Was the job site kept tidy, or did you find yourself picking up empty bottles and cigarette butts every evening?

- Was the professional easy to reach and responsive?

- And finally, the clincher: Would you hire this person again?

Once you've talked to the references and feel confident in their recommendation, do a follow-up interview with the contractor and ask more specific questions:

- Will the workers be there every day?

- What time does the workday start?

- Will the floors be covered, and if so, with what? (Masonite is more protective than paper.)

- What about the Dumpster—when will it arrive, where will it sit, and how often will it be emptied? (An overflowing Dumpster is an invitation for animal visits.)

- Where will the portable toilets be positioned?

- Where will the workers eat lunch? (Be considerate of your neighbors; you want to make sure the debris and trucks don't spill over to neighboring yards or sight lines.)

- Can a weekly walk-through be arranged—a time to go over outstanding issues and flag upcoming concerns? If the contractor expresses reluctance, it might indicate that he is either too busy for a weekly meeting or not organized enough for that kind of exercise. My advice: Look for someone else.

Button Down
the Bids

At the same time you're checking references and visiting sites, you need to solicit the bids—the projected cost of the job. These are the experts' estimates on what it will take to design or build the project. If you're planning to use an architect, find out what fee structure he or she uses; some architects work by percentage of overall budget (10 to 20 percent), others charge a fixed amount, and some charge hourly. Also determine whether the architect is planning to bring in his own contractor, in which case he'd be responsible for that bid. More likely, you'll be the one doing the legwork to find the contractor, and you'll get the most accurate bid if you have the architect's plan in hand.

It's hard for a contractor to give you a real number if the scheme is still abstract or vague, leaving too much room for interpretation and thus variations in cost. The contractor needs to know that you are planning on bumping out, for example, or replacing windows and doors. Preferably, your architect will have already specified the manufacture and style of window so you can get an even more specific price.

Ideally, you want to give the same plan to three contractors simultaneously so you can compare apples to apples. Allow three to four weeks for a contractor to get back to you—a complete workup takes time. Bids come in one of two ways: a fixed price or a cost-plus. I prefer a fixed price bid—an agreed-upon all-inclusive number from the outset that prevents huge surprises later on, barring major changes you decide to make or unforeseen complications, like the need for a new septic system. If this happens, you have to make adjustments with a so-called change order (this is basically an addendum to the contract that details the new work and its cost). With a cost-plus bid, you pay as you go for time and materials, plus 15 to 20 percent profit on the overall cost of the job. Some homeowners, especially experienced ones, prefer this arrangement, since it lets them know what each and every tile and plank costs. The downside is that with no cap, costs can really escalate.

If the bids vary widely (in swings of tens of thousands of dollars), it's a sign that the scope of work is not clearly defined—and it's back to the drawing board with your kitchen designer or architect. Conversely, if the bids come in within a few hundred dollars of one another, then your architect or designer did a good job in drawing up your plan, and those particular contractors are good at interpreting specs—which bodes well for their expertise.

When comparing bids, don't get lost in the itemized numbers but rather focus on the bottom line. While one contractor's price for flooring may be high, perhaps his allowance for plumbing is on the low side. In any case, all contractors leave themselves wiggle room in the budget. They know there's a good chance they'll overlook an item or two or have to pay more than anticipated for one thing or another, so they create a hidey-hole to stash extra for the extras.

If one of the bids comes in lower—tantalizingly lower—than the others, make sure you double-check the references. You don't want the out-of-work desperate contractor just because he costs less; he may be out of work for a reason. (A good contractor, by contrast, is almost always busy, and you usually need to get on his dance card months in advance of a start date.) If a couple of bids come in very close and the references for both check out, then go with your gut. You're going to be dealing with this person day in and day out for quite a while.

TRADE TIP

One way to shave money from the overall budget is to do some of the sourcing and buying yourself—called *B/O* ("by owner"). The most common items owners purchase are appliances, tile, cabinets, lighting fixtures, and countertops. Compare the best prices you find to what the contractor, who likely has a wholesale discount, comes up with in his bid. You might beat him—or not.

Before the building begins, have the crew take a few precautions to assure that the rest of your home stays relatively pristine during construction.

- Protect neighboring rooms. Hang plastic sheeting, securely anchored, between rooms.

- Station a box of foot wipes (available at home improvement stores) at every interior and exterior door to stop dirt and debris from seeping through air vents, walls, and so on.

- Load up with heavy-duty trash cans for contractors to dump their lunch remains and other refuse.

- Cover floors with Masonite (a heavy, inexpensive linoleum-like material). Cover neighboring floors with paper, or dust will seep into cracks.

- Remove personal belongings that might be damaged by dust and construction debris from the kitchen and neighboring rooms.

- Set up the garage to receive large deliveries.

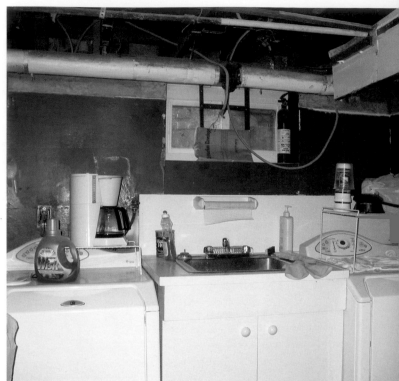

[ABOVE LEFT] UNINTENDED CONSE-QUENCES: REPLACING THE FENCE WASN'T IN THE GAME PLAN; NOW IT IS!

[ABOVE RIGHT] THE BASEMENT MIGHT NOT BE THE IDEAL SPOT FOR A TEMPORARY KITCHEN, BUT IT'S BET-TER THAN DOING WITHOUT. FIND A CONVENIENT SPOT WITH WASTE AND WATER LINES.

[RIGHT] YOUR ON-SITE CARPENTRY WILL BE DONE, WELL, ON SITE. FIND OUT WHERE YOUR CAST AND CREW INTEND TO SET UP SHOP.

Visit the Vendors

Even if you've a hired a designer, you're going to want to put your eyes (and hands) on the many kitchen options out there in the marketplace—the appliances, the cabinetry and countertops, the handles and faucets and hinges. Plan on taking several trips, either solo or with your designer, significant other, or someone you trust, to showrooms, stores, and marble yards to get ideas, take pictures, and gather samples and brochures to mull over later.

In my experience, it's a good idea to take a photo of a stone or a tile, or to take home samples—of not just your first and favorite but also your second and third choices. You may find yourself bumping the third choice up to first if your budget suddenly tightens or your family weighs in with a different opinion. Sometimes, too, time changes your mind. After a while, you might decide you are willing to go with a less expensive cabinet—maple recessed doors rather than walnut raised panels, for example—so you won't have to compromise on your state-of-the-art stove. Simply living with a sample for a few days or a few weeks may influence your final decision. You may think you're committed to the rich red stone countertop for the island, but the more you look at the simplicity of the plain gray sample, the more its subtlety may appeal.

Should You Stay or Should You Go?

This is the question every renovator has to answer. Clearly, installing new appliances doesn't require moving the family to a rental, but a major remodeling in which walls are knocked down and floors ripped up may require an exit strategy. There are two schools of thought about living in the house during construction. Proponents say there's no substitute for being on site all the time, especially first thing in the morning, to answer questions and oversee the work and workers—plus, they argue, the rental money is better spent on the renovation itself. Detractors contend that moving out allows the construction process to move along more speedily (without you and your family underfoot) and that, in fact, the cost saved by a quicker completion outweighs the cost of a rental.

My feeling on the matter is that while living through an entire house renovation is masochistic, staying put during a kitchen project is feasible—as long as you can close the door on the noise and the mess and can set up a temporary kitchen elsewhere in the house, a modest expense compared to moving to a rental. If you know your regular kitchen is going to be out of commission for several months, try to create your makeshift kitchen in a room that backs up to the kitchen, laundry room, or any other room with a water line. See if you can have a plumber tap into the water pipe through a small hole in the plaster so you can set up a sink— perhaps the old one, appropriated from the kitchen under demolition. The water pressure may not be as strong as you're used to, but it will be adequate to wash dishes. The cost of jury-rigging a temporary sink is certainly worth it, considering the annoyance of scrubbing pots in the tub or finding bloated Froot Loops in the bathroom sink. Along with a sink, you'll likely want a fridge

[BELOW] YOUR RENOVATION MAY BE BELOW STAIRS, BUT DUST AND SOOT WILL FILTER THOUGH THE HEAT AND AIR SYSTEM—THROUGH THE VERY WALLS BLANKETING THE ENTIRE HOUSE.

(either the old one plugged into a corner or a mini dorm-style one), a microwave, or a hot plate and electric skillet—and a base cabinet or two (borrowed from the "before" kitchen as well) to provide a work surface and a bit of storage space.

While a cleverly arranged temporary kitchen allows you to cook simple meals, it may not take the heat off of living in a construction zone. Even the best relationships and most easygoing families are tested by a renovation. One client of mine, a mother of preschoolers, confided sotto voce that three months in a house without a real kitchen had sent her and her husband into marriage counseling! In deciding whether to stay or move out, you need to think about your own threshold of stress as well as events or sea changes that will be going on in your family's life at that time—such as starting a new job or helping a child deal with college applications. No renovation is worth living through if it's going to put you over the edge!

Know What to Expect When

The pace of a kitchen project is slow overall, but the work does progress in a logical and predictable fashion. The first phase, the demolition, is actually the fastest part, and it's highly rewarding—euphoric, even—to witness the almost instantaneous change in the space. With a renovation, it's not uncommon for the demo crew to get down to the studs in a matter of a day or two. In new construction, the thrill comes in seeing the framing go up. Suddenly you can see your structure. But beware of false hope at this point. The rest of the construction process slows down—way down.

The second phase—preparing the kitchen for its new surfaces—is the most prolonged part of the job. This stage includes reinforcing the subfloor to support new stone, adding insulation, running heat, and plumbing, all of which take time—allow up to six weeks for these installations. Adding to the slowdown is a series of

[RIGHT] THIS KITCHEN IS ALMOST THIRTY YEARS OLD, YET THE TERRA-COTTA FLOOR STILL LOOKS FRESH AND UP-TO-DATE. WHEN INVESTING IN A KITCHEN, BE SURE YOUR CHOICES CAN STAND THE TEST OF TIME BOTH IN TERMS OF STYLE AND DURABILITY.

municipal inspections of the plumbing and electrical work, for which you may have to wait; building departments often have a backlog of inspections on their roster. Be sure to find out when these inspections are scheduled, so you can be present and hear firsthand whether or not you've passed that hurdle. (An aside: I find that some contractors use delayed inspections as an excuse to scoot off to another job site for a while, bringing your job to a standstill—another version of "the dog ate my homework." Press your contractor to work on some part of the project that can progress without the inspection, such as framing, windows, or insulation.)

The fun starts again with the installation phase, during which the contractor lays down the floor, unpacks your cabinets, and slides appliances into place. Now your war zone starts to take shape, and you must be vigilant. Ask the workers to use padded dollies and wear paper booties over their work shoes to trek heavy-duty appliances and banks of cabinets across the new floors. Be sure they watch out while maneuvering around the just-hung door moldings. The last installations are usually the kitchen counter and sink, followed by the backsplash.

To keep a kitchen renovation on schedule, you have to do your part, too. If your contractor says he needs a decision on a floor material, paint color, or knob choice by such-and-such a date, don't dither. If you let one deadline slip past, you may end up slowing everything down and paying for the delays. It behooves you to stay on top of the schedule if you want to stay on budget.

Go with the Flow

Construction is not a science but rather a fluid process. You can have 98 percent of a kitchen project nailed down, and certain unknowables will still pop up.

There are three things no contractor can control: what's behind the walls, the weather, and you. Most projects entail some awful moment of discovery: You can't straighten out the refrigerator wall after all because a chimney is in the way. Or the subfloor is completely rotted, or the exterior walls are bowed. One day, when I was on site with a client, the electrician ordered us to evacuate the kitchen immediately because he'd found exposed electrical wires behind the cabinets.

How you resolve unforeseen conditions and challenges depends on the degree of the damage or obstacle and how willing you are to make major (money-sapping) modifications. Sometimes you have no choice, as with a rotten subfloor or bad wiring, which *must* be fixed. But you could opt to forgo moving the refrigerator rather than mucking around with the location of the flue. Remember, too, that if you approve major construction fixes or change orders, it will affect the entire schedule; for example, you may need to delay your appliance or cabinet delivery.

Granted, certain change orders are unavoidable, but others are optional and fall into the as-long-as-you're-here category. It's not unlike being in a clothing shop and deciding to get new shoes to go with your new pants. Perhaps you had decided you'd simply live with your existing moldings; they looked fine. Well, maybe they did against the peeling counters and decrepit cabinets, but once you replace those elements, the moldings might suddenly look small and tired, and you may decide you want to trade those in (and up), too. Unless you're the rare type who can resist every temptation to change your mind or change the plan, I advise you to pad the budget a tad so you can give in to a few impulse decisions.

Even with the best-laid plans and the most experienced team, a mistake or two is inevitable. Perhaps you decided to install a door between the entry and the kitchen and now the light switch for the entry is hard to get to. As soon as you spot an oversight, flag it. The longer you wait, the

higher the cost; it's much easier to fix a mistake when the walls are still open than to wait until the Sheetrock is up and the walls are painted.

[ABOVE] A SUREFIRE WAY TO KEEP COSTS UNDER CONTROL IS TO RE-TAIN SOME OF WHAT YOU ALREADY HAVE. IT'S NOT ALL OR NOTHING. NEW CABINETS MARRY WELL WITH THE ORIGINAL CABINETS. THE TREND TOWARDS MISMATCHED CABINETRY IS LIBERATING—ALMOST ANYTHING GOES.

To keep track of the normal shifts in a budget, get the change orders in writing. Renovators often experience sticker shock at the end of the project, when all of the extras are totaled, remembering only that their contractor said, "Oh, that won't cost much." Add up all those "that's," and you've got significant cost overruns. Weekly meetings with the contractor are also imperative. Use them to go over change orders, check the schedule, and edit or adjust design details—as well as expectations.

Most often at your weekly walkthrough it will be you and the contractor—you with your list of questions and concerns and him with his list of reasons and justifications, as well as new suggestions. To make the meeting productive and keep the lines of communication clear and open, be organized. Have an agenda with a list of questions categorized by trade: plumbing, electrical, flooring. Give your contractor a heads-up the day before about what you want to address in the meeting, in case he wants to have a specific tradesperson present, such as the electrician. Jot down any comments about completion and delivery dates, and update your notes at each subsequent meeting.

Above all, throughout the renovation or construction, maintain your sense of humor. And keep your eye on the prize: a great working, living, breathing kitchen.

RESOURCES

If you've done as many design projects as I have, you come to know the best resources for outfitting a kitchen, from the big-ticket items (appliances and cabinets) to the smallest details (tile and hardware). Here's a comprehensive list.

Appliances

AGA
802-253-9727
www.aga-ranges.com
Costs a pretty penny but delivers a specialized look. Ovens are on the small side.

AMANA
800-843-0304
www.amana.com
Affordable pro-style appliances. Fridge with bottom freezer consistently ranked the best in the built-in and regular-depth category.

ARISTON
888-426-0845
www.aristonappliances.us
A new kid on the block with a full range of affordable appliances.

ASKO
800-898-1879
www.askousa.com
The king of energy efficiency—the only appliance manufacturer to get an endorsement from Greenpeace. Specializing in dishwashers and laundry equipment.

BOSCH
800-921-9622
www.boschappliances.com
Dependable, high-quality, reliable. Many chic, sleek units to choose from at various price points.

DACOR
800-793-0093
www.dacor.com
Personal favorite wall ovens for looks and longevity. They marry well with other cooktops. Now has new line of dishwashers, refrigeration products, and built-in coffee machine centers.

DE'LONGHI
866-844-6566
www.delonghimajorappliances.com
Ranges with range, as in a pro-style stove with warming drawers and a 36-inch pro-style range with two ovens.

ELMIRA STOVE WORKS
800-295-8498
www.elmirastoveworks.com
Great source for vintage looks and modern function.

FISHER AND PAYKEL
800-863-5384
www.fisherpaykel.com
The premier dishwasher drawers, made in New Zealand (now serviced under the KitchenAid label).

FIVE STAR
423-476-6544
www.fivestarrange.com
One of the original pro-style ranges for the home—and one of the best.

FRIGIDAIRE
800-444-4944
www.frigidaire.com
Still the most reasonably priced stainless-steel appliance packages around.

GAGGENAU
800-828-9165
www.gaggenau-usa.com
European company, owned by Bosch—caters to Euro sizing and sensibility.

GARLAND
717-636-1000
www.garlandgroup.com
The real-deal restaurant-style range—sturdy and hardworking.

GENERAL ELECTRIC
800-626-2000
www.geappliances.com
Go for the top-end Monogram line—good quality, good looks in a range of styles.

INSINKERATOR
800-558-5700
www.insinkerator.com
The king of garbage disposals. Get batch loading activator.

JENN-AIR
800-536-6247
www.jennair.com
High-end line of the Maytag family—especially good for secondary appliances, such as the indoor cooktop grill.

KITCHENAID
800-422-1230
www.kitchenaid.com
The least expensive built-in refrigeration of good quality and the best and the biggest of the American-made dishwashers.

LA CORNUE
www.lacornue.com
Big money for big-statement stoves in a luscious range of colors.

LG APPLIANCES
800-243-0000
www.lgusa.com
Innovative Korean company with many appliances making a run for the U.S. market (some parts are hard to replace).

LIEBERTS ROYAL GREEN APPLIANCE CENTER
914-428-5363 (phone ahead for an appointment)
aesposito@lrgappl.com
228 East Post Road
White Plains, NY 10601
Simply the best appliance showroom I've ever been to for choice, quality, and advice.

MARVEL
800-428-6644
www.lifeluxurymarvel.com
Great source for all kinds of wine refrigerators and undercounter refrigerators.

MAYTAG

800-688-9900

www.maytag.com

Not just a washing machine any more. Parent company of Amana, Magic Chef, and Jenn-Air. Models often share design features.

MIELE, INC.

800-843-7231

www.miele.com

Pricy, but people love these German-made dishwashers (with exclusive upper-level silverware basket) and washing machines. Least service calls of any dishwasher I've encountered.

NORTHLAND

www.northlandnka.com

Refrigeration specialists. Offers unique sizes and features (like glass doors) for refrigerators and wine coolers.

SCOTSMAN

847-215-4500

www.scotsman-ice.com

Better known in the commercial market for its undercounter refrigerators, ice makers, and wine coolers, but also available for residential usage.

SHARP

800-237-4277

www.sharpusa.com

Makes most microwaves on the market.

SUB-ZERO

www.subzero.com

800-222-7820

The original built-in refrigerator, available in many sizes (and the only one on the market with two compressors). Parent company of Wolf and as high-end as you can get.

THERMADOR

800-656-9226

www.thermador.com

An American-made appliances company (double wall ovens and cooktops are the specialty), owned by Bosch. Great value.

U-LINE

414-354-0300

www.u-line.com

Family-owned Wisconsin company specializing in undercounter refrigeration, ice makers, and refrigerator and wine cooling drawers.

VIKING RANGE CORP.

888-845-4641

662-455-1200

www.vikingrange.com

The gold standard for pro-style ranges for the home. Available in various widths and custom colors. Surprisingly, no more expensive than the competition.

VULCAN

502-778-2791

www.vulcanhart.com

High-powered range for serious—that is, usually commercial—use.

WASTE KING
800-767-6293
www.anaheimmfg.com
Powerful kitchen sink waste disposers for residential as well as commercial use.

WHIRLPOOL
800-253-3977
www.whirlpool.com
A broad spectrum of reliable options, from dishwashers to refrigerators to mictowaves, including energy-saving Energy Star models. Winner of the 2006 Sustained Excellence Award from Energy Star.

WOLF APPLIANCES
608-271-2233
www.wolfappliance.com
Expensive and high-quality line of ranges, warming drawers, wall ovens, and cooktops. Owned by Sub-Zero.

Sinks and Faucets

AMERICAN STANDARD
800-752-6292
www.americanstandard-us.com

BARCLAY PRODUCTS LTD.
847-244-1234
www.barclayproducts.com

BATES AND BATES
562-808-2290
www.batesandbates.com

BEST PLUMBING TILE AND STONE
914-723-2002
www.bestplg.com
830 Central Avenue
Scarsdale, NY 10583

BLANCO
800-241-3184
www.blancosink.com

THE CHICAGO FAUCET COMPANY
847-803-5000
www.chicagofaucets.com

DELTA FAUCET CO.
800-345-DELTA
www.deltafaucet.com

DORNBRACHT USA, INC.
800-774-1181
www.dornbracht.com

ELKAY
630-572-3192
www.elkay.com

FRANKE
800-626-5771
www.franke.com

HANSGROHE
770-360-9880
www.handsgrohe-usa.com

HARRINGTON BRASS WORKS
201-818-1300
www.harringtonbrassworks.com

KOHLER CO.
800-456-4537
www.kohler.com

MOEN
800-553-6636
www.moen.com

RENOVATOR'S SUPPLY
800-922-5507

SAMUEL HEATH AND SONS
www.samuel-heath.com

Hoods and Vents

BROAN
800-558-1711
www.broan.com

NUTONE
888-336-3948
www.nutone.com

VENT-A-HOOD
972-235-5201
www.ventahood.com

Cabinetry

BILOTTA KITCHENS OF MOUNT KISCO
914-242-1022
www.bilotta.com
175 Main Street
Mt. Kisco, NY 10549

CHRISTOPHER PEACOCK BESPOKE
ENGLISH CABINETRY
203-862-9333
4 Deerfield Drive
Greenwich, CT 06830

CRAFTSMAN KITCHENS
801-293-8001
3591 South 300 West
Salt Lake City, UT 84115

CROWN POINT
800-999-4994
www.crown-point.com

EXPO DESIGN CENTER
www.expo.com

FUHRMANN KITCHENS, INC.
914-698-3300
253 Halstead Avenue
Mamaroneck, NY 10543

IKEA
www.ikea.com

KENNEBEC COMPANY
www.kennebeckcompany.com

KITCHENS BY DEANE, INC.
203-327-7008
1267 E. Main Street
Stamford, CT 06902

KRAFTMAID CABINETRY
800-654-3008
www.kraftmaid.com

PLAIN AND FANCY CUSTOM CABI-
NETRY
800-447-9006
www.plainfancycabinetry.com

QUALITY CUSTOM CABINETRY
717-656-2721
www.qcc.com

RUTT HANDCRAFTED CABINETRY
717-351-1700
www.ruttcabinetry.biz

WOOD-MODE, INC.
570-374-2711
www.wood-mode.com

Cabinetry Hardware

AMEROCK CORPORATION
800-435-6959
www.amerock.com

BALDWIN HARDWARE CORPORATION
800-566-1986
www.baldwinhardware.com

CROWN CITY HARDWARE
www.crowncityhardware.com

LIZ'S ANTIQUE HARDWARE
323-939-4403
www.lahardware.com

RESTORATION HARDWARE
800-910-9836
www.restorationhardware.com

TOP KNOBS
800-499-9095
www.topknobsusa.com

VAN DYKES RESTORERS
800-558-1234
www.vandykes.com

Cabinet Storage Amenities

REV-A-SHELF
502-499-1126
www.rev-a-shelf.com

CUSTOM INSERTS
877-4-CUSTOM
www.custominserts.com

Countertops

AVONITE SURFACES
800-428-6648
www.avonitesurfaces.com

CAESARSTONE QUARTZ SURFACES
818-394-6000
www.caesarstoneus.com

DUPONT CORIAN
800-426-7426
www.corian.com

FORMICA CORPORATION
800-367-6422
www.formica.com

MARBLE MODES, INC.
718-539-1334
15-25 130th Street
College Point, NY 11356

MILLENNIUM STONE
914-939-0999
1 Mill Street
Port Chester, NY 10573

PETRILLO STONE CORP.
914-668-8561
610 S. Fulton Avenue
Mount Vernon, NY 10550

STONE SOURCE
www.stonesource.com

SILESTONE
800-291-1311
www.silestone.com

VERMONT SOAPSTONE CO.
800-263-5404
www.vermontsoapstone.com

WILSONART
800-433-3222
www.wilsonart.com

Tile

ANN SACKS
212-463-8400
800-278-8453
www.annsacks.com
5 E. 16th Street
New York, NY 10003

CARMINART, INC.
914-592-6330
61 Saw Mill River Road
Elmsford, NY 10523

COUNTRY FLOORS
12 East Putman Avenue
Greenwich, CT 06830
www.countryfloors.com

DAL-TILE CORP.
214-398-1411
www.daltile.com

PARIS CERAMICS
312-467-9830
www.parisceramics.com

PORCELANOSA
www.porcelanosa-usa.com

WALKER ZANGER
877-611-0199
www.walkerzanger.com

WATERWORKS
www.waterworks.com

Wood Floors

BAMBOO HARDWOODS
www.bamboohardwoods.com

GEYSIR HARDWOOD FLOORS
914-381-4100

GOODWIN HEART PINE
www.heartpine.com

HOBOKEN FLOORS
www.hobokenfloors.com

MANNINGTON WOOD FLOORS
910-884-5600

PERGO FLOORING
919-773-6000

Linoleum and Cork

ARMSTRONG FLOORS
www.armstrongfloors.com

CONGOLEUM CORP.
609-584-3000
www.congoleum.com

GLOBUS CORK
www.corkfloor.com

MARMOLEUM
www.forbo-flooring.com

TARKET, INC.
610-266-5500

Lighting

HALO LIGHTING
www.haloltg.com

LIGHTOLIER
508-679-8131
www.lightolier.com

MOTIF DESIGNS
800-431-2424
www.motif-designs.com

REJUVENATION
888-401-1900
www.rejuvenation.com

URBAN ARCHEOLOGY
www.urbanarcheology.com

VAUGHAN
www.vaughandesigns.com

Dimmers and Wall Plates

LUTRON
888-588-7661
www.lutron.com

Overall Kitchen Resources

INTERNATIONAL CODE COUNCIL
www.intlcode.org

NATIONAL KITCHEN AND BATH ASSO-CIATION
800-NKBA-PRO
www.nkba.org

CREDITS

Cynthia Chang and Brian Scanlan's Kitchen (see page xii)

ALEX KAALI-NAGY DEVELOPMENT CORP. (ARCHITECT)
70 Pine Street
New Canaan, CT 06840
203-966-8254
www.kaali-nagy.com

FORM LIMITED KITCHEN AND BATH DESIGN
Mark Musayev
32 West Putnam Avenue
Greenwich, CT 06830
203-869-6880
www.formlimited.com

ROBIN CHRISTINE INTERIOR DESIGN
56 Valley Terrace
Rye Brook, NY 10573
914-329-8191

Dishwasher: Bosch
Ovens and cooktop: Thermador
Refrigerators: Sub-Zero

Jessica and Lou Marinaccio's Kitchen (see page 33, top)

M. A. S. CONSTRUCTION CO. (CONTRACTOR)
914-699-0226

Kristiina Ratia's Kitchen (see pages 102–103)

KRISTIINA RATIA DESIGNS
815 Post Road
Darien, CT 06820
203-852-0027

Cabinets: Custom
Cooktop: Viking
Dishwasher: Bosch
Ovens: Miele
Refrigerator: Sub-Zero
Warming drawers: Viking

Beth and Kevin Mullaney's Kitchen (see pages 58–59)

CHRISTOPHER POWELL (ARCHITECT)
212-645-7180

LYN PETERSON (DESIGNER)
Motif Designs
718 South Fulton Avenue
Mount Vernon, NY 10550
www.motif-designs.com

Cabinets: Craftsman Kitchens
Dishwasher: Miele
Refrigerator: Sub-Zero
Stove: Wolf
Trash compactor: KitchenAid
Warming drawer: Thermador

Nancy and Jim Utaski's Kitchen (see pages ii–iii)

FAIRFAX AND SAMMONS (ARCHITECT)

Lyn Peterson and Karl Friberg's Kitchen
(see page 143)

LYN PETERSON (DESIGNER)
Motif Designs
718 South Fulton Avenue
Mount Vernon, NY 10550
www.motif-designs.com

Cooktop: Russell Range
Ovens: Thermador
Refrigerator: Sub-Zero
Dishwasher: Bosch

Raymond Waites and Russell Burge's Kitchen
(see page xi, top)

RAYMOND WAITES DESIGN, INC.
230 Fifth Avenue #1200
New York, NY 10001
212-447-8700
www.raymondwaites.com

Architect: John Nolis
Appliances: Viking
Cabinets: American Classic
Kitchens/Woodmode

William Cummings and Bernt Heiberg's Kitchen (see page 28)

HEIBERG CUMMINGS DESIGN (ARCHITECT)
9 West Nineteenth Street #3
New York, NY 10011
212-337-2030
www.hcd3.com

Appliances: GE
Cabinets: Milled at Timehari
Plate Racks: hcd3.com collection

John Dransfield and Jeffrey Ross's Kitchen
(see pages 40–41)

DRANSFIELD & ROSS (DESIGNERS)
John Dransfield and Jeffrey Ross
54 West Twenty-First Street
New York, NY 10010
www.dransfieldandross.biz
212-741-7278

RICHARD WARD BAXTER RESTORATIONS INC. (CABINETMAKER)
P.O. Box 1919
Amagansett, NY 11930
516-527-3897

Appliances: GE Monogram

Sue and Mort Fuller's Kitchen (see pages 138–139)

CROZIER GEDNEY ARCHITECTS, P.C. (ARCHITECT)
41 Elm Place
Rye, NY 10580
914-967-6060

Jill and Ken Iscol's Kitchen (see pages 98–99)

KRISTIINA RATIA DESIGNS
815 Post Road
Darien, CT 06820
203-852-0027

Dishwasher: Miele
Cabinets: Custom
Freezer: Sub-Zero
Refrigerator: Sub-Zero
Stove: Viking

Kat and Chris Burki's Kitchen (see page 136)

KAT BURKI INTERIORS
340 Pequot Avenue
Southport, CT 06890
203-254-2908

Cabinets: Custom
Dishwasher: Miele
Refrigerator: Sub-Zero
Stove: Viking
Wine cooler: Sub-Zero

Ty Stapleton's Kitchen (see pages 124–125)

STAPLETON DESIGN GROUP
168 The Prado
Atlanta, GA 30309
404-483-3675

Additional Kitchens

Acknowledgments

To the *New York Times* home section for labeling me the "kitchen girl" twenty-five years ago and consigning me to what I naïvely thought was the drudgery of designing kitchens. Now kitchen design seems like the most important slice of life—and decorating.

To my family: My husband, Karl Friberg; my children, Amer, Kris, Erik, and PF; and my new son-in-law, Cullen McMahon. I think I am the luckiest woman in the world to have you all. I know I am.

To the ever-changing but seemingly never-shrinking gang at the family campground: Uncle Bob; my nephew Graham White; my sister Chris Peterson; her husband, Peter Spader; and my sister-in-law Paula Friberg—ain't we got fun?

To my ever-patient (and very persistent) editor, Aliza Fogelson. You made Real Life Kitchens so very much better. Sincerest thanks.

To the rest of the cast and crew at Clarkson Potter:

Lindsay Miller—you are always a pleasure

Selina Cicogna—a phone call from you is always good news

Marysarah Quinn—chic, cool, and completely capable

Jennifer K. Beal—your photography degree serves you well; thank you for my incredible design

To my agent, Carla Glasser, for her equanimity and good judgment.

To Susan Carlton, who turns my nonsense into good sense. Her spirit brightens my day, her phrases echo in my ears, and her homes inhabit my pages. And to Coco Myers, whom I already appreciate and admire, even if our relationship is thus far only electronic. These are two accomplished writers and editors.

To Robert Grant and Curtis Lew. What fun it is to still shoot with you so many years on. You are gifted photographers and very agreeable daymates.

To my stylist, my friend, my sleepover date, Kristiina Ratia, the most stylish woman alive.

To Sara Giovanitti, from whom I will never stop learning and whose take on everything I will never stop wanting to hear.

To Diana McMahon, my pinch-hit picture taker, I am thankful to have a photographer in the family.

To BJ Sharpe, my summer sister, my super-smart support system, my eternal source of info and accuracy. Everything she does she does exactly perfectly right, with integrity and an admirable inner strength.

To my cohorts at Motif Designs: Fran, Gayle, Darcie, Charles, Kelly, Mary, Katharine, Lisa, Keith, Ron, Ricardo, Alma, and Carmen Loarca—a paradigm.

Thank you all so very much for your aid and support—and for tolerating me—the "whirling dervish."

INDEX

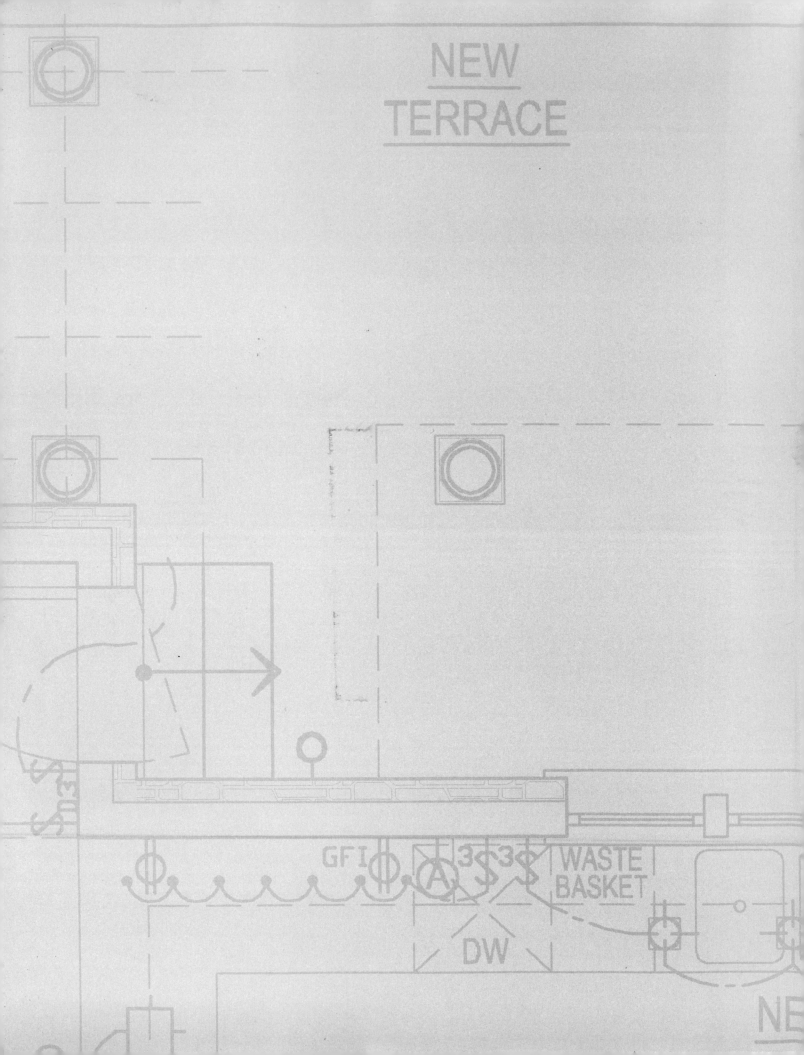

NEW
TERRACE

GFI 3 3 WASTE
BASKET
Ⓐ
DW

NE